PEARL

POETRY

Paper Aeroplane: Selected Poems 1989–2014
The Death of King Arthur: A New Verse Translation
Seeing Stars
Tyrannosaurus Rex Versus the Corduroy Kid
Sir Gawain and the Green Knight: A New Verse Translation
The Universal Home Doctor
Travelling Songs
Selected Poems
Killing Time
CloudCuckooLand
The Dead Sea Poems
Moon Country: Further Reports from Iceland (with Glynn Maxwell)
Book of Matches
Kid
Xanadu
Zoom!

DRAMA

The Story of the Iliad:
A Dramatic Retelling of Homer's Epic and the Last Days of Troy
The Odyssey: A Dramatic Retelling of Homer's Epic
Jerusalem
Mister Heracles (after Euripides)

PROSE

Walking Away
Walking Home: A Poet's Journey
Gig: The Life and Times of a Rock-star Fantasist
The White Stuff
Little Green Man
All Points North

PEARL

A New Verse Translation

SIMON ARMITAGE

LIVERIGHT PUBLISHING CORPORATION

a Division of W. W. Norton & Company

INDEPENDENT PUBLISHERS SINCE 1923

NEW YORK • LONDON

For information about permission to reproduce selections from
this book, write to Permissions, Liveright Publishing Corporation,
a division of W. W. Norton & Company, Inc.,
500 Fifth Avenue, New York, NY 10110

For information about special discounts for bulk purchases, please
contact W. W. Norton Special Sales at specialsales@wwnorton.com
or 800-233-4830

Manufacturing by RR Donnelley Harrisonburg
Book design by Brooke Koven
Production manager: Julia Druskin

ISBN 978-0-87140-718-4

W. W. Norton & Company, Inc.
500 Fifth Avenue, New York, N.Y. 10110
www.wwnorton.com

W. W. Norton & Company Ltd.
Castle House, 75/76 Wells Street, London W1T 3QT

1 2 3 4 5 6 7 8 9 0

To Susan Elizabeth and Emmeline Olivia

Introduction

EARTBROKEN and in mourning, a man describes the terrible sorrow he feels at the loss of his beautiful and irreplaceable "Perle." In August, with flowers and herbs decorating the earth and perfuming the air, he visits a green garden, the scene of his bereavement. Tormented by images of death and decay, devastated by grief and overpowered by the intoxicating scent of the plants, he falls into a sudden sleep and begins to dream, embarking on an out-of-body experience that will lead to an encounter with his departed pearl, who we learn is his child, and a journey to the gates of heaven.

Probably composed in the 1390s, only one copy of the untitled poem that has come to be called *Pearl* remains in existence. It was originally housed in the library of Henry Savile of Bank, in Yorkshire, then later in a collection belonging to Sir Robert Cotton, and is now held in the British Library as MS Cotton Nero A.x (each bookcase in Cotton's library was overlooked by a bust of a famous historical figure, including several Roman emperors). *Pearl* is the first poem in a manuscript that also includes *Sir Gawain and the Green Knight*, *Patience*, and *Cleanness* (or *Purity*). All four poems are in the same hand, and although the writing probably belongs to that of a scribe rather than the original author, most scholars believe they were composed by the same person, about whom we know very little. The historical context leads us to assume he was a man, and from the content of the poems we can deduce that he was well educated, well read, and very well acquainted with the Bible, though not necessarily a man of the cloth. The same type of linguistic sleuthing that proves the author to be a contemporary of Chaucer also suggests he was a native of the English Midlands or the North West, and both his language and his literary style are very different from his metropolitan counterpart. Chaucer's strain of Middle English is closer to today's speech and much of his vocabulary can be grasped or guessed at, whereas the vocabulary of the *Pearl-* or *Gawain*-poet is at times completely foreign to the modern reader, and may well have been somewhat obscure or antiquated even in its day. Theories and countertheories have developed around the identity of the *Pearl*-poet, some based on the subject matter of the poems, others on dialect words within them, but the truth is that the author of MS Cotton Nero A.x remains a mystery. What isn't in dispute, however, is his brilliance as a poet, and it is a sobering lesson to any writer that the name of someone so adept in the art can simply vanish from history.

Although less than half the length of *Sir Gawain and the Green Knight, Pearl,* in my view and in my experience, represents a greater challenge to the translator, largely because of the poem's unique form and intricate structure. Presented in twenty sections, each section consists of five stanzas of twelve lines, except for section XV which consists of six stanzas, bringing the total number of lines to an enigmatic 1212, thus mimicking not only the number of lines in each stanza but also the structure of the heavenly Jerusalem (twelve by twelve furlongs), with twelve gates for the twelve tribes of Israel, as specified in the Book of Revelation. Such number symbolism is indicative of a recursive symmetry practiced throughout the poem. The work is alliterative, often boasting three alliterating syllables per line, for example: "To clanly clos in golde so clere" (line 2), and although the poem doesn't have a strict meter or rhythm, most lines are constructed around four beats or stresses (that is to say, four emphasized syllables occur within each line). The lines are particularly compact and intense; *Sir Gawain and the Green Knight* is also made up of (arguably) four-beat lines but is noticeably "wider" on the page by comparison, suggesting that the author of *Pearl* was consciously fashioning a highly ornate and detailed piece, more lyrical than his other works, though one that still required all the necessary components of narrative. The echoing, sonic qualities of the poem brought about by alliteration are heightened through use of repetition, or "concatenation," in which a word or phrase in the last line of the first stanza in each section is repeated in the first and last line of each stanza throughout that section, then once more in the first line of the following section, thus producing a sort of poetic passing of the baton. To complete the effect, the opening line of the poem is recalled in its final line, representing a circularity or spherical endlessness reminiscent of a pearl stone itself. Some of the repeated words or phrases operate as puns or homonyms in the original, for example the word "mone" used throughout section XVIII, which can mean either moon or month. "Deme," in section VI, has multiple meanings (e.g., judge, estimate), and in cases such as this, where no direct contemporary equivalent exists, the latter-day translator is faced with some hard choices. The same is true where the original definition is difficult to pin down, as with "adubbemente" in section II, which has been translated variously as adornment, splendor, wonderment, embellishment, and (by me) ornament. Each of those definitions might seem to be little more than a minor variation on a theme, but choosing one, then working it into the text on nine further occasions, has serious ramifications for the words that precede and follow.

But the biggest dilemma concerns the principal technique by which the poem operates, namely that of rhyme, with each stanza adhering to a strict rhyme scheme of ababababbcbc. Some translators have stuck to the rhyme scheme by preserving many of the poem's original end words, most of which are archaic to the modern reader or even obsolete (e.g., "spenned," "sweven"). Some, like Marie Borroff, have made use of old-fashioned terms such as "demesne," "descried," and "agleam," then manipulated the surrounding sentence structure so as to position those rhyme words at the end of lines. Others have introduced new material into the poem in order to complete acoustic partnerships. For example, Tolkien offers "I vow that from over orient seas" as line 3 to chime with "please" at the end of line 1, yet as nifty as his solution appears, line 3 actually reads, "Oute of Oryent, I hardyly saye," (roughly: in all the Orient, I confidently say), with no mention at all of the sea. A more radical approach is to forgo all the formalities of the original and aim for something far more impressionistic, a version rather than a translation, with all the associated excitements and disappointments. Or to sacrifice the harmonies of the poem in pursuit of literal definitions, thereby securing a more faithful rendition, semantically speaking, but offering an impoverished poetic experience lacking atmosphere and character. I draw attention to the shortcomings of these different methodologies not out of criticism but out of sympathy. While working on the poem, every decision feels like a trade-off between sound and sense, between medieval authenticity and latter-day clarity, and between the precise and the poetic. My own response has been to allow rhymes to occur as naturally as possible within sentences, internally or at the end of lines, and to let half-rhymes and syllabic rhymes play their part, and for the poem's musical orchestration to be performed by pronounced alliteration, looping repetition, and the quartet of beats in each line. So formalists and technicians scanning for a ladder of rhyme words down the right-hand margin of this translation will be frustrated, though hopefully my solution will appeal to the ear and the voice.

So what is *Pearl* about? Notice is given from early on in the poem that the pearl is both a jewel and a young girl, referred to as "it" and "her," both a prized object and a beloved child. However, readers should not expect the poem to develop straightforwardly into an extended metaphor or "conceit." Because although the young woman has pearl-like qualities—paleness, purity, radiance—from the moment she reveals herself to the dreamer she is very much a person, albeit a spirit version of her earthly existence, an apparition. (In fact at line 483 we discover she "lyfed not two yer," so has become in death a being capable of mature thought and articulate speech.) She is the dreamer's maiden, his girl, nearer to him than "aunte or nece;" so by implication his daughter, though interestingly that particular word is never actually used. What follows is a dialogue, conducted between bereft father and deceased child across an unfordable stretch of water, in which the girl eventually explains how heaven is now her home and that she stands beside Christ Himself, as one of his brides. At first overjoyed, then incredulous, and at times skeptical that his pearl should have risen to such exalted heights, the dreamer is eventually persuaded by the force and persistence of the girl's argument and by the evidence of his own eyes. Toward the end of the poem, the girl presents an almost hallucinatory description of the palace of heaven, outlining its opulent geological foundations, its dazzling architecture and its glorious inhabitants, and invites the dreamer to steal a glimpse of the magnificent citadel. Awestruck by such a tantalizing prospect, the dreamer rushes forward to join his pearl on the other side of the water, leaping from the riverbank only to be jolted awake, and for the vision to break, and for his loved one to disappear once again. His grief has not lessened and he still swoons with longing. But through the lessons of scripture, delivered ironically from the mouth of his own lost child, he has arrived at a philosophical acceptance of his earthly predicament. *Pearl* is a poem of consolation, a reminder of the life that waits, especially for those who place spiritual values over cherished possessions. It begins and ends in a real garden, framing a visit to a more extraordinary paradise where the dreamer's outlook is transformed by the depth and power of the revelation.

So on one level the poem is a lesson in Christian doctrine, crammed from beginning to end with biblical allusions. Some are subtle and fleeting; some are reported almost verbatim, as with the repeated references to the Book of Revelation (or "the Apocalypse" as it appears in the poem); others are recounted and explicated in full, such as the Parable of the Vineyard (Matthew 20:1–16) which occupies six of the poem's stanzas. The Parable of the Pearl of Great Price (Matthew 13:45–46) might be thought of as the catalyst for the entire poem.

But *Pearl* is also a tense, fascinating, and at times extremely poignant duologue, especially if viewed as one between an actual father and his daughter, and the extent to which the poem is drawn from autobiographical circumstances is another matter for speculation. The dream vision as a method of religious instruction was certainly a well-established poetic convention of the period, providing a similar starting point for Langland's *Piers Plowman*, for example. Equally, encounters with characters from the afterlife have always been staples of myth, and a generative literary device in a tradition that includes Dante, Virgil, Ovid, and Homer. Yet the poem has the *feel* of the real, as if genuine grief provided the impetus for such a poetic undertaking, or as if a desire to describe and share the solace brought about through faith and spiritual reasoning had encouraged the author to broadcast his experience through the written word. The presentation of the poem in the first person—not an automatic choice for writers of the day by any means—reinforces the suggestion that the poem deals with personal history and a lived experience. Tolkien, in the introduction to his translation, repeats Sir Israel Gollancz's notion that "the child may have been actually called a pearl by baptismal name, Margarita in Latin, Margery in

English. It was a common name at the time, because of the love of pearls and their symbolism, and it had already been borne by several saints." If the poem is nothing more than an invented allegory, then I salute its creator and readily admit to being moved by the fiction, not least at the misplaced elation the dreamer experiences when he believes himself reunited with his child, the emotions of which I found harder to bear than the weight of the grief. And if true sorrow and anguish do lie behind the poem, then as the parent of one child—a daughter—I offer this translation in memory of the lost pearl, as a tribute to the poetic courage of her father, and as an act of condolence.

—SIMON ARMITAGE

PEARL

I

1

Perle plesaunte to Prynces paye,
To clanly clos in golde so clere!
Oute of Oryent, I hardyly saye,
Ne proved I never her precios pere,
So rounde, so reken in uche araye,
So smal, so smothe her sydez were.
Queresoever I jugged gemmez gaye,
I sette hyr sengeley in syngulere.
Allas! I leste hyr in on erbere;
Thurgh gresse to grounde hit fro me yot.   10
I dewyne, fordolked, of luf-daungere,
Of that pryvy perle wythouten spot.

I

I

Beautiful pearl that would please a prince,
fit to be mounted in finest gold,
I say for certain that in all the East
her precious equal I never found.
So radiant and round, however revealed,
so small, her skin so very smooth,
of all the gems I judged and prized
I set her apart, unparalleled.
But I lost my pearl in a garden of herbs;
she slipped from me through grass to ground,   10
and I mourn now, with a broken heart,
for that priceless pearl without a spot.

9. Song of Solomon 4:12: "My sister, my spouse, is a garden enclosed, a garden
enclosed, a fountain sealed up."
11. Song of Solomon 2:5: "Stay me up with flowers, compass me about with
apples: because I languish with love."
12–60. Revelation 14:5: "And in their mouth there was found no lie; for they are
without spot before the throne of God."

2

Sythen in that spote hit fro me sprange,
Ofte haf I wayted, wyschande that wele
That wont watz whyle devoyde my wrange,
& heven my happe & al my hele,
That dotz bot thrych my hert thrange,
My breste in bale bot bolne & bele.
Yet thoght me never so swete a sange
As stylle stounde let to me stele;   20
Forsothe ther fleten to me fele,
To thenke hir color so clad in clot.
O moul, thou marrez a myry juele,
My privy perle wythouten spotte!

3

That spot of spysez mot nedez sprede,
Ther such rychez to rot is runne;
Blomez blayke & bluwe & rede
Ther schynez ful schyr agayn the sunne;
Flor & fryte may not be fede
Ther hit doun drof in moldez dunne;   30
For uch gresse mot grow of graynez dede,
No whete were ellez to wonez wonne;
Of goud uche goude is ay bygonne;

2

And in that spot where it sprang from me
I've often watched, wishing for the one
that drove away sorrow, lightened my load,
roused my spirits and rallied my health.
Loss and longing lean on my heart
and my breast burns with the heat of the hurt;
yet no song was ever as sweetly sung
as the silent moments that stole me away   20
on the many occasions she came to mind.
To think of her color, now clad in clods . . .
oh black soil, you blot and spoil
my precious pearl without a spot.

3

Spices must thrive and spread in that spot
where rot and ruin enrich the soil;
blooms of white and blue and red
turn shining faces toward the sun.
Flower and fruit could never fade
where my pearl entered the dark earth;   30
grasses must grow from lifeless grains
or wheat would never be brought to the barn.
For goodness out of goodness is born,

---

31. John 12:24–25: "Amen, amen I say to you, unless the grain of wheat falling into the ground die, itself remaineth alone. But if it die, it bringeth forth much fruit. He that loveth his life shall lose it; and he that hateth his life in this world, keepeth it unto life eternal."

So semly a sede moght fayly not,
That spryngande spycez up ne sponne
Of that precios perle wythouten spotte.

4

To that spot that I in speche expoun
I entred, in that erber grene,
In Auguste in a hygh seysoun,
Quen corne is corven wyth crokez kene.   40
On huyle ther perle hit trendeled doun
Schadowed this wortez ful schyre & schene—
Gilofre, gyngure, & gromylyoun,
& pyonys powdered ay bytwene.
Yif hit watz semly on to sene,
A fayr reflayr yet fro hit flot,
Ther wonys that worthyly, I wot & wene,
My precious perle wythouten spot.

5

Bifore that spot my honde I spenned
For care ful colde that to me caght;   50
A devely dele in my hert denned,
Thagh resoun sette myseluen saght.
I playned my perle that ther watz spenned
Wyth fyrte skyllez that faste faght;
Thagh kynde of Kryst me comfort kenned,

and such a seed couldn't fail to root
nor splendid spices sprout and shoot
from that precious pearl without a spot.

4

I went to the spot my words describe,
entered the garden green with herbs
in the month of August on holy day,
when corn succumbs to the sharpened scythe.   40
That pearl had rolled away from a mound
where brightly lit plants cast bold shadows:
ginger, gromwell and gillyflower
with peonies scattered in between—
such a sweet scene for the eye to see,
made fairer by fragrances floating up . . .
I believe and know where that lovely one lives,
my precious pearl without a spot.

5

In that same spot I clasped my hands,
wholly overcome by the coldness of sorrow.   50
A desolating grief had gripped my heart
when reason could have put my mind at rest.
I pined for my pearl in its earthen prison
and fierce thoughts fought back and forth;
though the nature of Christ offered me comfort

My wreched wylle in wo ay wraghte.
I felle upon that floury flaght,
Suche odour to my hernez schot;
I slode upon a slepyng-slaghte—
On that precios perle wythouten spot.   60

my wretched desire writhed in despair.
Among those flowers I fell to the floor,
my senses suddenly swamped by scent,
and sank into heavy sleep on the ground
where my pearl was lost, on the same spot.   60

II

6

Fro spot my spyryt ther sprang in space,
My body on balke ther bod in sweven;
My goste is gon in Godez grace,
In aventure ther mervaylez meven.
I ne wyste in this worlde quere that hit wace,
Bot I knew me keste ther klyfez cleven;
Towarde a foreste I bere the face,
Where rych rokkez wer to dyscreven.
The lyght of hem myght no mon leven,
The glemande glory that of hem glent;   70
For wern never webbez that wyghez weven
Of half so dere adubbemente.

7

Dubbed wern alle tho downez sydez
Wyth crystal klyffez so cler of kynde.
Holte-wodez bryght aboute hem bydez
Of bollez as bluwe as ble of ynde;
As bornyst sylver the lef onslydez,

II

6

Suddenly my spirit rose from that spot,
while in body I remained asleep on the mound,
and by God's grace my spirit embarked
on a quest to where marvel and amazement happen.
I couldn't say where I was in the world,
but my soul was set down where cliffs split the sky
and I turned my face toward a forest
where astounding stones astonished the eye:
no one would believe what light they lent,
what gleaming glory shone from them;   70
never on this earth did a human hand
weave cloth so exquisite in ornament.

7

Ornamenting the hills to every side
were crystal cliffs of the clearest form;
in and about stood bright-colored woods—
trees with trunks of Indian blue.
Layers of leaves like burnished silver

That thike con trylle on uch a tynde
Quen glem of glodez agaynz hem glydez;
Wyth schymeryng schene ful schrylle thay schynde.   80
The gravayl that on grounde con grynde
Wern precious perlez of Oryente;
The sunnebemez bot blo & blynde
In respecte of that adubbement.

8

The adubbemente of tho downez dere
Garten my goste al greffe forghete;
So frech flavorez of frytez were
As fode hit con me fayre refete.
Fowlez ther flowen in fryth in fere,
Of flaumbande huez, bothe smale & grete;   90
Bot sytole-stryng & gyternere
Her reken myrthe moght not retrete;
For, quen those bryddez her wyngez bete,
Thay songen wyth a swete asent;
So gracios gle couthe no mon gete
As here & se her adubbement.

9

So al watz dubbet on dere asyse
That fryth ther fortune forth me ferez.
The derthe therof for to devyse
Nis no wyz worthe that tonge berez.   100
I welke ay forth in wely wyse;

shivered and shook on every bough;
when clear daylight glided across them
they glinted and glimmered with a dazzling gleam.   80
The grinding gravel which crunched underfoot
was precious pearl of the Orient,
so even sunbeams seemed dark and dim,
outshone by opulent ornament.

8

The image of highly ornamented hills
made my spirit forget all feelings of grief.
The air was so fresh with the scent of fruit
it nourished and fed me as if it were food.
All shape and size of shimmering fowl
flocked and flew as one through the wood;   90
no stringed instrument making its sound
could mimic the glorious music they made:
when they beat their wings, out of those birds
came a song of heavenly harmony.
What person could hope for a pleasure more pure
than to hear and see their ornament?

9

Where rich ornament was arrayed all around
I followed as Fortune led me through a forest;
no tongue could tell of its true nature
for in beauty and wonder it went beyond words.   100
In a state of ecstasy I strolled along,

No bonk so byg that did me derez.
The fyrre in the fryth, the feirer con ryse
The playn, the plonttez, the spyse, the perez,
& rawez & randez & rych reverez—
As fyldor fyn her bonkes brent.
I wan to a water by schore that scherez;
Lorde, dere watz hit adubbement!

10

The dubbemente of tho derworth depe
Wern bonkez bene of beryl bryght;   110
Swangeande swete the water con swepe,
Wyth a rownande rourde raykande aryght;
In the founce ther stonden stonez stepe,
As glente thurgh glas that glowed & glyght
As stremande sternez, quen strothe men slepe,
Staren in welkyn in wynter nyght;
For uche a pobbel in pole ther pyght
Watz emerad, saffer, other gemme gente,
That alle the loghe lemed of lyght,
So dere watz hit adubbement.   120

no bank high enough to prove a barrier.
Flowers were fairer the further I went,
among sedges, shrubs, spices and pears,
hedges, wetlands and splendid streams
with steep slopes like spun gold,
and arrived at the shore of a winding river,
overwhelming, oh Lord, in its ornament.

10

At the water's edge, ornamenting its depths,
were bountiful banks of bright beryl.   110
The surface swirled as it swept by,
pouring forward, murmuring as it flowed.
And the bed was studded with brilliant stones,
glinting and glowing like light through glass,
as radiance streams from distant stars
in the winter sky while the world sleeps.
Because every pebble set into that pool
was an emerald or sapphire or another jewel;
the river looked luminous along its length
so gleaming were those gem-like ornaments.   120

107. Revelation 22:1–2: "And he shewed me a river of water of life, clear as crys-
tal, proceeding from the throne of God and of the Lamb. In the midst of the
street thereof, and on both sides of the river, was the tree of life, bearing twelve
fruits, yielding its fruits every month, and the leaves of the tree were for the
healing of the nations."

III

11

The dubbement dere of doun & dalez,
Of wod & water & wlonk playnez,
Bylde in me blys, abated my balez,
Fordidden my stresse, dystryed my paynez.
Doun after a strem that dryghly halez
I bowed in blys. Bredful my braynez;
The fyrre I folwed those floty valez,
The more strenghthe of joye myn herte straynez.
As fortune fares ther as ho fraynez,
Whether solace ho sende other ellez sore,   130
The wyz to wham her wylle ho waynez
Hyttez to have ay more & more.

12

More of wele watz in that wyse
Then I cowthe telle thagh I tom hade;
For urthely herte myght not suffyse
To the tenthe dole of tho gladnez glade.
Forthy I thoght that paradyse

III

11

The ornamented dazzle of downs and dales,
of wood and water and splendid meadows
infused me with bliss, eased my burdens,
soothed my sorrows and dispelled my hurt,
and I followed that freely flowing stream,
light-headed with elation, alive with joy.
Venturing further through brook-filled valleys
my spirit gained strength with every step;
when Fortune puts a person to the test
by offering solace or ordering suffering   130
the person she turns her attention toward
finds more of either pleasure or pain.

12

There was more splendor displayed in that scene
than time would ever allow me to tell,
and a human heart could hardly hold
one tenth of the rapturous gladness it aroused.
I felt, therefore, that Paradise itself

Watz ther over gayn tho bonkez brade;
I hoped the water were a devyse
Bytwene myrthez by merez made;   140
Beyonde the broke, by slente other slade,
I hope that mote merked wore.
Bot the water watz depe, I dorst not wade,
& ever me longed ay more & more.

13

More & more, & yet wel mare,
Me lyste to se the broke beyonde;
For if hit watz fayr ther I con fare,
Wel loveloker watz the fyrre londe.
Abowte me con I stote & stare,
To fynde a forthe faste con I fonde;   150
Bot wothez mo iwysse ther ware,
The fyrre I stalked by the stronde;
& ever me thoght I schulde not wonde
For wo ther welez so wynne wore.
Thenne newe note me com on honde,
That meved my mynde ay more & more.

14

More mervayle con my dom adaunt;
I saw beyonde that myry mere
A crystal clyffe ful relusaunt;
Mony ryal ray con fro hit rere.   160
At the fote therof ther sete a faunt,

must be there beyond those broad banks,
and supposed the stream a border of sorts,
a dividing line through lovely lands,   140
and that somewhere over the shore of the brook
I would find the site of its walled city.
The water was deep and I didn't dare wade,
but more and more I longed to cross.

13

That longing mounted, till more than ever
I desired to see beyond the stream,
and though it was wonderful here where I walked
it appeared more wonderful over the water.
I stopped and stared, surveyed my surroundings,
impatient to find a fording place,   150
but the dangers were great, and grew greater
the further I strayed along the strand.
I told myself not to hesitate,
to fear no harm in those happy acres,
but a curious image now caught my eye
which moved my mind more and more.

14

A more marvelous matter amazed me now:
beyond that beautiful water I witnessed
a crystal cliff, brilliantly bright,
radiant with glorious gleaming rays,   160
and seated at the foot of that summit was a child,

A mayden of menske ful debonere;
Blysnande whyt watz hyr bleaunt—
I knew hyr wel, I hade sen hyr ere—
As glysnande golde that man con schere,
So schon that schene anunder schore.
On lenghe I loked to hyr there,
The lenger I knew hyr more & more.

15

The more I frayste hyr fayre face,
Her fygure fyn, quen I had fonte,   170
Suche gladande glory con to me glace
As lyttel byfore therto watz wonte.
To calle hyr lyste con me enchace,
Bot baysment gef myn hert a brunt;
I saw hyr in so strange a place,
Such a burre myght make myn herte blunt.
Thenne verez ho up her fayre frount,
Hyr vysayge whyt as playn yvore,
That stonge myn hert ful stray atount,
& ever the lenger, the more & more.   180

a noble girl, a young woman of grace,
wearing a gown of iridescent white.
And I knew her so well—I had seen her before.
Like sawn gold that glistens inside
she sat at the base of the cliff, and she shone.
I stared, astonished, and the longer I looked
the more I recognized and remembered her.

15

The more I focused on her fine face
and gazed in awe at her graceful form,   170
waves of exultant emotion overwhelmed me
with a force like nothing I'd felt before.
Love encouraged me to call out her name
but shock had sent a hammer-blow to my soul;
to see her there, in such strange surroundings
had stunned my senses, almost stopping my heart.
Then she lifted her head toward the light,
and her face was so fine and ivory-white
that its wonder stung me. I stood there bewildered,
as if mezmerised for evermore.   180

---

163. Revelation 19:8: "And it is granted to her that she should clothe herself with
fine linen, glittering and white. For the fine linen is the justification of saints."

IV

16

More then me lyste my drede aros;
I stod ful stylle & dorste not calle,
Wyth yghen open & mouth ful clos;
I stod as hende as hawk in halle.
I hope that gostly watz that porpose;
I dred onende quat schulde byfalle—
Lest ho me eschaped that I ther chos,
Er I at steven hir moght stalle.
That gracios gay wythouten galle,
So smothe, so smal, so seme slyght,   190
Rysez up in hir araye ryalle,
A precios pyece in perlez pyght.

17

Perlez pyghte of ryal prys
There moght mon by grace haf sene,
Quen that frech as flor-de-lys
Doun the bonke con boghe bydene.

IV

16

More in alarm than out of longing
I stood spellbound, unable to speak,
my eyes transfixed but my tongue frozen,
as hushed and watchful as a hawk in a hall.
This appearance, I thought, is an apparition,
and fear held me: how would I feel
if the vision before me vanished from view
without contact or closeness occurring between us?
Oh blissful one, oh unblemished soul,
so flawless, fragile, so flatteringly slender.   190
Then she rose up in resplendent robes,
a precious being in priceless pearls.

17

Priceless pearls, imperially worn,
were a marvelous sight, a miracle to the eye,
her figure as vivid as fleur-de-lys
as she walked forward toward the water.

Al blysnande whyt watz hir bleaunt of biys,
Upon at sydez, & bounden bene
Wyth the myryeste margarys, at my devyse,
That ever I saw yet with myn yghen;   200
Wyth lappez large, I wot & I wene,
Dubbed with double perle & dyghte,
Her cortel of self sute schene,
Wyth precios perlez al umbepyghte.

18

A pyght coroune yet wer that gyrle,
Of marjorys & non other ston,
Highe pynakled of cler quyt perle,
Wyth flurted flowrez perfet upon.
To hed hade ho non other herle;
Her here-leke al hyr vmbegon.   210
Her semblaunt sade for doc other erle,
Her ble more blaght then whallez bon;
As schorne golde schyr her fax thenne schon,
On schylderez that leghe unlapped lyghte.
Her depe colour yet wonted non
Of precios perle in porfyl pyghte.

Her fine linen shone luminously white,
open at the sides, every hem stitched
with fabulous pearls—more stunning by far
than any my eyes had fixed on before.   200
And if memory serves, her flowing sleeves
were adorned with pearls set down in pairs,
and her matching gown glowed like morning,
proudly apparelled with priceless pearls.

18

That princess wore a priceless crown
studded with pearls and no other stones,
pure clear pearls arranged in pinnacles
among figures of expertly fashioned flowers.
She wore no other circlet or headdress
but her wimple fully encircled her face,   210
her expression as earnest as a duke or earl,
her complexion whiter than the bone of a whale.
Loosely hanging, her hair lay lightly
around her shoulders, shining like spun gold,
and the almost transparent appearance of her pallor
compared well with those priceless pearls.

197. Revelation 19:8: "And it is granted to her that she should clothe herself with
fine linen, glittering and white. For the fine linen is the justification of saints."

19

Pyght & poyned watz uche a hemme,
At honde, at sydez, at overture,
Wyth whyte perle & non other gemme,
& bornyste quyte watz hyr vesture.   220
Bot a wonder perle wythouten wemme
In myddez hyr breste watz sette so sure.
A mannez dom moght dryghly demme
Er mynde moght malte in hit mesure;
I hope no tong moght endure
No saverly saghe say of that syght,
So watz hit clene & cler & pure,
That precios perle ther hit watz pyght.

20

Pyght in perle, that precios pyece
On wyther half water com doun the schore;   230
No gladder gome hethen into Grece
Then I quen ho on brymme wore;
Ho watz me nerre then aunte or nece;
My joy forthy watz much the more.
Ho profered me speche, that special spece,
Enclynande lowe in wommon lore,
Caghte of her coroun of grete tresore,
& haylsed me wyth a lote lyghte.
Wel watz me that ever I watz bore,
To sware that swete in perlez pyghte!   240

19

Her priceless wristband and the pretty hems
at her collar, cuffs and open neck
were lined with pearls and pearls alone;
everything she wore was wondrously white.   220
But one pearl especially took pride of place,
burnished and unblemished, positioned at her breast;
the man who attempted to imagine its magnitude
would find himself flummoxed, his mind befuddled.
In truth, no tongue could ever tell
a sensible syllable about that stone,
so clean and proud and clear and pure,
unparalleled even among priceless pearls.

20

In her priceless pearls that precious girl
arrived at the river on the opposite reach.   230
No man was gladder from here to Greece
than I was, to watch her at the water's edge.
She was nearer to my heart than an aunt or niece
and my love for her fierce and limitless.
Then that special being spoke to me:
she inclined low with a ladylike curtsy,
removed the exquisite crown from her head
and with grace and courtesy greeted me.
What a blessing to be born just to speak with that girl,
dressed and adorned in priceless pearls.   240

V

21

'O perle,' quod I, 'in perlez pyght,
Art thou my perle that I haf playned,
Regretted by myn one, on nyghte?
Much longeyng haf I for the layned,
Sythen into gresse thou me aglyghte;
Pensyf, payred, I am forpayned,
& thou in a lyf of lykyng lyghte,
In paradys erde, of stryf unstrayned.
What wyrde hatz hyder my juel vayned,
& don me in thys del & gret daunger?   250
Fro we in twynne wern towen & twayned,
I haf ben a joylez juelere.'

V

21

'Oh pearl, in those priceless pearls,' I said,
'are you really my pearl, whose passing I mourn,
and grieve for alone through lonely nights?
Endless sorrow I have suffered and endured
since you slipped from my grasp to the grassy earth;
I am hollow with loss and harrowed by pain,
yet here you stand, lightened of all strife,
at peace in the land of Paradise.
What fate has led my pearl forward
and positioned me here to feel such pain?   250
Entwined once, now torn from our twinship
I live without joy like a jeweler without jewel.'

241–300. Matthew 13:45–46: "Again, the kingdom of heaven is like to a merchant seeking good pearls, who, when he had found one pearl of great price, went his way, and sold all that he had, and bought it."

22

That juel thenne in gemmez gente
Vered up her vyse wyth yghen graye,
Set on hyr coroun of perle orient,
& soberly after thenne con ho say:
'Sir, ye haf your tale mysetente,
To say your perle is al awaye,
That is in cofer so comly clente,
As in this gardyn gracios gaye,   260
Hereinne to lenge for ever & play,
Ther mys nee mornyng com never nere;
Her were a forser for the in faye,
If thou were a gentyl jueler.

23

'Bot, jueler gente, if thou schal lose
Thy joy for a gemme that the watz lef,
Me thynk the put in a mad porpose,
& busyez the aboute a raysoun bref;
For that thou lestez watz bot a rose
That flowred & fayled as kynde hyt gef;   270
Now thurgh kynde of the kyste that hyt con close
To a perle of prys hit is put in pref.
& thou hatz called thy wyrde a thef,
That oght of noght hatz mad the cler,
Thou blamez the bote of thy meschef,
Thou art no kynde jueler.'

22

Then that jeweled one in her noble gems
looked up and gazed with those gray-blue eyes,
put on her crown of oriental pearls
and spoke without sentiment, saying to me:
'Sir, there's no truth in what you say.
You lament that your pearl is lost for ever
when the exquisite coffer encasing her
is this wonderful garden and glorious estate,   260
and here is her home for eternity
where misery and melancholy never come near.
What worth this casket would truly hold
if measured and judged by a master jeweler.

23

'But my gentle jeweler, if you are dejected
at the loss of a gem which lent you such joy,
then your mind pursues a mad purpose
and troubles itself with a trifling cause.
What rendered you bereft was only a rose
that flowered and faded as nature intended.   270
But now, through the nature of the chest where it lies,
its worth as a precious pearl is proven.
And you falsely infer your fate is a thief,
when He conjures you something from nothing, quite clearly.
Since you heap blame on the healing balm
I judge you to be no natural jeweler.'

24

A juel to me then watz thys geste,
& juelez wern hyr gentyl sawez.
'Iwyse,' quod I, 'my blysfol beste,
My grete dystresse thou al todrawez.   280
To be excused I make requeste;
I trawed my perle don out of dawez;
Now haf I fonde hyt, I schal ma feste,
& wony wyth hyt in schyr wod-schawez,
& love my Lorde & al his lawez,
That hatz me broght thys blys ner;
Now were I at yow beyonde thise wawez,
I were a joyful jueler.'

25

'Jueler,' sayde that gemme clene,
'Wy borde ye men so madde ye be?   290
Thre wordez hatz thou spoken at ene;
Vnavysed, forsothe, wern alle thre;
Thou ne woste in worlde quat on dotz mene,
Thy worde byfore thy wytte con fle.
Thou says thou trawez me in this dene,
Bycawse thou may wyth yghen me se;
Another thou says, in thys countre
Thyself schal won wyth me ryght here;
The thrydde, to passe thys water fre,
That may no joyfol jueler.   300

24

That visitor was a jewel to me then, a vision
whose noble words were no less gemmed.
'Oh best and blessed one,' I said to her,
'you dispel my grief and great distress,   280
so I ask you please to pardon me
for believing my pearl was oblivion's prize.
Now that I've found it again I'll rejoice,
and dwell with that beauty in the bright dells,
and love my Lord and all His laws
who has brought blissfulness back to me.
To join you beyond this wide water
would make this man a joyful jeweler.'

25

'Jeweler,' that glittering gem then said,
'why must men joke? You must all be mad.   290
Three utterances you issued all at once,
each as null and empty as the next.
What meaning they have must escape the man
whose mouth moves ahead of his mind.
Firstly, you feel you have found me in this valley
having seen the evidence with your own eyes.
Secondly, you state you will stay right here,
and live your life alongside me in this land.
Thirdly, you think you will bridge this brook—
no gentle jeweler could make such a journey.   300

VI

26

'I halde that jueler lyttel to prayse
That lovez wel that he saw wyth yghe,
& much to blame & vncortayse
That levez oure Lorde wolde make a lyghe,
That lelly hyghte your lyf to rayse,
Thagh fortune dyd your flesch to dyghe.
Ye setten hys wordez ful westernays
That levez nothynk bot ye hit syghe;
& that is a poynt o sorquydryghe,
That uche god mon may evel byseme,   310
To leve no tale be true to tryghe
Bot that hys one skyl may dem.

27

'Deme now thyself if thou con dayly
As man to God wordez schulde heve.
Thou saytz thou schal won in this bayly;
Me thynk the burde fyrst aske leve,
& yet of graunt thou myghtez fayle.

VI

26

'I judge unworthy of praise the jeweler
who only believes what his eyes behold,
and call him discourteous and worthy of blame
for believing our Lord would speak a lie,
who faithfully promised to lift up your life
should Fortune cause your flesh to rot.
You set the words of our Saviour askew
by clinging to the saying that seeing is believing,
an expression of a person's love of pride.
It is unbecoming in a courteous man   310
to try and to test but trust no truth
beyond those facts which flatter his judgment.

27

'Now judge for yourself if you have spoken
in the manner a man should address the Almighty.
You say out loud you will live in this land—
I think you must plead for permission first,
and such a favor could well be refused.

Thou wylnez over thys water to weve;
Er moste thou cever to other counsayl;
Thy corse in clot mot calder keve;   320
For hit watz forgarte at paradys greve,
Oure yorefader hit con mysseyeme;
Thurgh drewry deth boz uch man dreve,
Er over thys dam hym Dryghtyn deme.'

28

'Demez thou me,' quod I, 'my swete,
To dol agayn, thenne I dowyne.
Now haf I fonte that I forlete,
Schal I efte forgo hit er ever I fyne?
Why schal I hit bothe mysse & mete?
My precios perle dotz me gret pyne!   330
What servez tresor bot garez men grete
When he hit schal efte wyth tenez tyne?
Now rech I never for to declyne,
Ne how fer of folde that man me fleme,
When I am partlez of perle myne.
Bot durande doel what may men deme?'

29

'Thow demez noght bot doel-dystresse,'
Thenne sayde that wyght; 'why dotz thou so?
For dyne of doel of lurez lesse
Ofte mony mon forgos the mo;   340
The oghte better thyselven blesse,

And you wish to pass over this watercourse,
but first you must plot a different path:
your cold corpse must sink through the soil;   320
it was forfeited by our ancestor, Adam,
who misguarded it in the Garden of Eden.
Every man must experience cruel demise
before God in his judgment will grant the crossing.'

28

'Sweet one,' I pleaded, 'that judgment you pass
is a life sentence of sorrow and loss.
Now I have gained what I thought was gone
must I lose it again before my life's end?
Why must I find then forfeit my prize?
My priceless pearl, you inflict such pain.   330
What use is treasure if it leads to tears,
when its absence causes the heart to ache?
I'm indifferent now to how far I might fall
or the distance and depth to which I'm driven.
Deprived of my precious pearl I expect
a dark journey till my judgment day.'

29

'You judge your lot as dejection and hurt,'
said the gracious girl, 'Why is that so?
Through his lament for lesser losses
man often misses the greater gain.   340
Better to sign yourself with the cross

& love ay God, & wele, & wo,
For anger gaynez the not a cresse;
Who nedez schal thole, be not so thro.
For thogh thou daunce as any do,
Braundysch & bray thy brathez breme,
When thou no fyrre may, to ne fro,
Thou moste abyde that he schal deme.

30

'Deme Dryghtyn, ever hym adyte,
Of the way a fote ne wyl he wrythe;   350
Thy mendez mountez not a myte,
Thagh thou for sorghe be never blythe;
Stynt of thy strot & fyne to flyte,
& sech hys blythe ful swefte & swythe.
Thy prayer may hys pyte byte,
That mercy schal hyr craftez kythe;
Hys comforte may thy langour lythe,
& thy lurez of lyghtly leme;
For, marred other madde, morne & mythe,
Al lys in hym to dyght & deme.'   360

and thank your God through thick and thin,
because anger profits you not one penny.
If man must suffer he should sidestep stubbornness,
and instead of dancing like a cornered deer,
wriggling and writhing and bleating his woes
with no exit or escape either this way or that,
he should heed the judgment of God in heaven.

30

'Call Him unjust till the end of the Earth,
but He will not swerve by a single step.   350
No crumb of comfort will come your way
if you wallow and wail in the well of pity,
so quieten your quibbling, quit your carping
and swiftly and honestly seek His sympathy.
Hope that your prayers will pierce His heart,
so that mercy might do what mercy does best.
The comfort He offers can ease your anguish,
scatter your fears, put sorrow to flight,
so bury your feelings or flail in fury,
the Almighty alone is judge and jury.'   360

VII

31

Thenne demed I to that damyselle:
'Ne worthe no wraththe unto my Lorde,
If rapely I rave spornande in spelle.
My herte watz al wyth mysse remorde,
As wallande water gotz out of welle;
I do me ay in hys myserecorde.
Rebuke me never wyth wordez felle,
Thagh I forloyne my dere endorde,
Bot kythez me kyndely wyth your coumforde,
Pytosly thenkande upon thysse: 370
Of care & me ye made acorde,
That er watz grounde of alle my blysse.

32

'My blysse, my bale, ye han ben bothe,
Bot much the bygger yet watz my mon;
Fro thou watz wroken fro uch a wothe,

VII

31

With judicious words I said to my jewel:
'Let there be no offense to my Lord
if I rage and rave with spluttering speech.
But my heart is heavy and talk rushes headlong
like water from a spring, surging and spewing.
I fall on His mercy, this moment and for ever.
Never reproach me with wounding words
despite my errors, my gilded angel,
but kindly offer your consolations.
Be caring and thoughtful and recall this: 370
you who paired me with painful despair
were the bedrock on which my bliss was built.

32

'My bliss and my grief—you have been both—
but my grief has been the greater by far.
Since you were exiled from earthly care

365. Psalms 21:15: "I am poured out like water."

I wyste never quere my perle watz gon.
Now I hit se, now lethez my lothe.
&, quen we departed, we wern at on,
God forbede we be now wrothe,
We meten so selden by stok other ston.   380
Thagh cortaysly ye carp con,
I am bot mol & marerez mysse;
Bot Crystes mersy & Mary & Jon—
Thise arn the grounde of alle my blysse.

33

'In blysse I se the blythely blent,
& I a man al mornyf mate;
Ye take theron ful lyttel tente,
Thagh I hente ofte harmez hate.
Bot now I am here in your presente,
I wolde bysech wythouten debate   390
Ye wolde me say in sobre asente
What lyf ye lede erly & late;
For I am ful fayn that your astate
Is worthen to worschyp & wele iwysse;
Of alle my joy the hyghe gate,
Hit is in grounde of alle my blysse.'

34

'Now blysse, burne, mot the bytyde,'
Then sayde that lufsoum of lyth & lere;
'& welcum here to walk & byde,

I could not guess where my pearl had gone,
but seeing it again my sorrow subsides.
Once in harmony, we were torn in half;
may God forbid we be broken again,
we so seldom meet by tree or stone!   380
Though your conversation with me is courteous
I lack all manners and am little more than dust.
Let the mercy of Christ and Mary and John
be the base on which I build my bliss.

33

'You stand before me in a blissful state,
and myself a demoralized, mournful man.
You appear to notice nothing of this,
though I suffer greatly from searing sadness.
But since you appear in my presence here
I ask you to say, without argument,   390
and to answer my question with hand on heart,
what life you lead through dawn and dusk.
My spirit soars, knowing your position
is one of worth and high honor,
for this is the ground and this the gate
by which the road to my blissfulness runs.'

34

'May bliss find and follow you, sir,'
said that figure of lovely limb and face.
'You are welcome to walk and wait in this place,

For now thy speche is to me dere;   400
Maysterful mod & hyghe pryde,
I hete the, arn heterly hated here.
My Lorde ne lovez not for to chyde,
For meke arn alle that wonez hym nere,
& when in hys place thou schal apere,
Be dep devote in hol mekenesse;
My Lorde the Lamb lovez ay such chere,
That is the grounde of alle my blysse.

35

'A blysful lyf thou says I lede;
Thou woldez knaw therof the stage.   410
Thow wost wel when thy perle con schede
I watz ful yong & tender of age;
Bot my Lorde the Lombe, thurgh hys Godhede,
He toke myself to hys maryage,
Corounde me quene in blysse to brede
In lenghe of dayez that ever schal wage;
& sesed in alle hys herytage
Hys lef is, I am holy hysse;
Hys prese, hys prys, & hys parage,
Is rote & grounde of alle my blysse.'   420

for now your speech is pleasing to hear. 400
Arrogant attitude and haughty pride,
I have to tell you, are detested here.
My Lord has no liking of life's complainers
and only the humble find a home in His house.
When you come to rest at last in His realm
be deeply devout and meek in demeanor.
My Lord the Lamb, who loves such a manner,
is the rock on which my blissfulness rests.

35

'You say I lead a blissful life
and wonder at such an exalted existence. 410
As you know full well, when your pearl fell
I was young in years and innocent at heart.
But my Lord the Lamb by divine love
brought me to marriage and made me His bride,
crowned me His queen to bloom in blessedness
today and tomorrow, till eternity.
His honor and heritage I have inherited;
I am wholly His and His alone.
His grace, His nobility and family line
are the root and branch of all my bliss.' 420

VIII

36

'Blysful,' quod I, 'may thys be truwe,
Dysplesez not if I speke errour.
Art thou the quene of hevenez bluwe,
That al thys worlde schal do honour?
We leven on Marye that grace of grewe,
That ber a barne of vyrgynflour;
The croune fro hyr quo moght remuwe
Bot ho hir passed in sum favour?
Now for synglerty o hyr dousour,
We calle hyr Fenyx of Arraby,   430
That freles fleghe of hyr fasor,
Lyk to the Quen of cortaysye.'

37

'Cortayse Quen,' thenne sayde that gaye,
Knelande to grounde, folde up hyr face,
'Makelez Moder & myryest May,
Blessed Bygynner of uch a grace!'
Thenne ros ho up & con restay,

VIII

36

'My bliss,' I said, 'can your tale be true?
Don't take offense if I speak out of turn
by questioning if you are heaven's queen,
worshipped by everyone the world over.
We believe in Mary, mother of all grace,
who bore a child while pure and chaste.
No one could vie for the Virgin's crown
unless they surpassed her in some noble aspect.
Rare and unrivaled, unique in her sweetness,
she has come to be called the Phoenix of Arabia,   430
a peerless creature that flew from her Creator,
as did the queen of courtesy.'

37

'Courteous Queen,' said that lovely creature,
kneeling on the floor, raising her face,
'Matchless mother and fairest maid,
fount from which grace and goodness flows.'
Then from her prayers she stood and paused

& speke me towarde in that space:
'Sir, fele here porchasez & fongez pray,
Bot supplantorez none wythinne thys place;   440
That Emperise al hevenez hatz,
& urthe & helle in her bayly;
Of erytage yet non wyl ho chace,
For ho is Quen of cortaysye.

38

'The court of the kyndom of God alyve
Hatz a property in hyt self beyng:
Alle that may therinne aryve
Of alle the reme is quen other kyng,
& never other yet schal depryve,
Bot uchon fayn of otherez hafyng,   450
& wolde her corounez wern worthe tho fyve,
If possyble were her mendyng.
Bot my Lady, of quom Jesu con spryng,
Ho haldez the empyre over us ful hyghe;
& that dysplesez non of oure gyng,
For ho is Quene of cortaysye.

39

'Of courtaysye, as saytz Saynt Paule,
Al arn we membrez of Jesu Kryst;
As heved & arme & legg & naule
Temen to hys body ful truwe & tryste,   460
Ryght so is uch a Krysten sawle

and in that place she spoke these words:
'Sir, many seek grace and are granted it here,
but in this domain there are no usurpers.   440
All heaven belongs to that holy empress,
and earth and hell are within her dominion.
No one will oust her from her high office
for she is the queen of courtesy.

38

'The company of the court of God's kingdom
live by a custom unique to this country.
Everyone who arrives and enters here
is called the queen or king of the realm,
and no one person shall deprive another,
but derive pleasure from a neighbor's possessions   450
and wish their crowns were five-fold in worth
if such an improvement were possible.
But my lady, mother of Jesus our Lord,
she is highest of all throughout this empire,
and none of our company is sorry that is so,
for she is the queen of courtesy.

39

'And through such courtesy, as Saint Paul preaches,
we are all joined with Jesus Christ;
as head and arm and leg and navel
are firmly fastened to each person's frame,   460
so every single Christian soul

A longande lym to the Mayster of myste.
Thenne loke what hate other any gawle
Is tached other tyghed thy lymmez bytwyste;
Thy heved hatz nauther greme ne gryste,
On arme other fynger thagh thou ber byghe.
So fare we alle wyth luf & lyste
To kyng & quene by cortaysye.'

40

'Cortayse,' quod I, 'I leve,
& charyte grete, be yow among.   470
Bot my speche that yow ne greve,
. . . . .
Thyself in heven over hygh thou heve,
To make the quen that watz so yonge.
What more honour moghte he acheve
That hade endured in worlde stronge,
& lyved in penaunce hys lyvez longe,
Wyth bodyly bale hym blysse to byye?
What more worschyp moght he fonge,
Then corounde be kyng by cortaysye?   480

belongs to the Master of spiritual mysteries.
Could hate or similar sentiments exist
between one being's body parts?
Does your head experience anger or envy
if your wrist or finger flaunts a ring?
And like those limbs we live and love
among heaven's courteous queens and kings.'

40

'Courtesy,' I said, 'it seems certain,
and heartfelt charity are at home here.   470
But without offense let me offer these words:
*
If you really inhabit these rarefied heights
and became a queen while so young in years,
what high honor might be handed to him
who stood strong and steadfast through strife,
enduring penance through endless days
and earning his bliss through bodily ache?
Surely he would enter heaven with ease
and be crowned a king of courtesy?   480

*Line missing in original manuscript.

IX

41

'That cortayse is to fre of dede,
Ghyf hyt be soth that thou conez saye;
Thou lyfed not two yer in oure thede;
Thou cowthez never God nauther plese ne pray,
Ne never nawther Pater ne Crede.
& quen mad on the fyrst day!
I may not traw, so God me spede,
That God wolde wrythe so wrange away;
Of countes, damysel, par ma fay,
Wer fayr in heven to halde asstate,   490
Ather ellez a lady of lasse aray;
Bot a quene!—hit is to dere a date.'

42

'Ther is no date of hys godnesse,'
Then sayde to me that worthy wyghte,
'For al is trawthe that he con dresse,
& he may do nothynk bot ryght,
As Mathew melez in your messe,

IX

41

'Our gentle Lord acts too generously
if what you say is actually so.
You lived for less than two years in our world,
knew neither your creed nor paternoster
nor how to pray or to please God,
but were dubbed a queen on your first day!
My Lord excuse me, but I cannot believe
that God would make such a great mistake.
On my word, young woman, it would be one thing
if you were counted a countess of heaven   490
or allotted the role of a lower lady.
But a queen no less—that exceeds the limit.'

42

'There is no limit to our Lord's love,'
were that worthy woman's words to me,
'for all is honorable that He ordains,
and He practices nothing that is not pure,
as the message of Matthew in the mass reminds us

In sothfol Gospel of God Almyght;
In sample he can ful graythely gesse,
& lyknez hit to heven lyghte.
"My regne," he saytz, "is lyk on hyght   500
To a lorde that hade a vyne, I wate.
Of tyme of yere the terme watz tyght,
To labor vyne watz dere the date.

43

"'That date of yere wel knawe thys hyne.
The lorde ful erly up he ros,
To hyre werkmen to hys vyne,
& fyndez ther summe to hys porpos.
Into acorde thay con declyne
For a pene on a day, & forth thay gotz,   510
Wrythen & worchen & don gret pyne,
Kerven & caggen & man hit clos.
Aboute vnder the lorde to marked totz,
& ydel men stande he fyndez therate.
'Why stande ye ydel?' he sayde to thos;
'Ne knawe ye of this day no date?'

44

"'Er date of daye hider arn we wonne;'
So watz al samen her answar soght;
'We haf standen her syn ros the sunne,

in a true gospel of Almighty God.
That parable paints a fitting picture
which likens honor to the light of heaven.   500
"My kingdom on high," he explains, "is comparable
to the winemaker looking to hire his workers
at that time of the year when the date dictates
to labor at the vines until daylight's limit.

43

'"All laborers know that date is a limit.
So the vineyard owner rose very early
to take on hands to tend his estate,
and found a gang of able fellows,
men who would work in the fields for a wage
of a penny a day. With the pay agreed,   510
they toiled at the trying and tiring tasks,
trimming and tying, cultivating the crop.
At nine the master went back to the market
where men hung about, kicking their heels.
'Why wait here idle and aimless?' he asked,
'when the light of day is not limitless?'

44

'"'We came before sunrise, at night's limit,'
said the unemployed in unison.
'and we've waited here since the dawn of day,

501–72. Matthew 20:1–16: Parable of the Vineyard.

& no mon byddez us do, ryght noght.'   520
'Gos into my vyne, dotz that ye conne;'
So sayde the lorde, & made hit toght.
'What resonabele hyre be naght be runne,
I yow pay in dede & thoghte.'
Thay wente into the vyne & wroghte,
& al day the lorde thus yede his gate,
& newe men to hys vyne he broghte.
Welnez wyl day watz passed date.

45

'"At the date of day of evensonge,
On oure byfore the sonne go doun,   530
He saw ther ydel men ful stronge,
& sayde to hem wyth sobre soun:
'Wy stonde ye ydel thise dayez longe?'
Thay sayden her hyre watz nawhere boun.
'Gotz to my vyne, yemen yonge,
& wyrkez & dotz that at ye moun.'
Sone the worlde bycom wel broun;
The sunne watz doun, & hit wex late;
To take her hyre he mad sumoun;
The day watz al apassed date.   540

willing to work, but no one wants us.'
'Go to my land, begin your labors,'   520
said the master of the vineyard, making this vow:
'What wage you are due at the day's end
I promise to pay you—that is my pact.'
So they went to the vineyard and got to work,
and the lord of the manor went on in this manner,
bringing hired hands to the vines every hour
till the long day narrowed and neared its limit.

45

'"As day neared its limit, at evensong,
one hour before the sun goes down,   530
men were still milling about in the market,
and the vintner addressed them in a serious voice:
'Why loiter and idle all day long?'
They replied no employer had appointed them.
'Go to my land, young laborers,
and work at the vines as well as you can.'
And soon the world was shrouded in shadow,
the sun was lost and it was late.
As he summoned the workers to receive their wage
the day had lengthened and outlived its limit.   540

X

46

'"The date of the daye the lorde con knaw,
Called to the reve: 'Lede, pay the meyny;
Gyf hem the hyre that I hem owe;
& fyrre, that non me may repreny,
Set hem alle upon a rawe,
& gyf uchon inlyche a peny.
Bygyn at the laste that standez lowe,
Tyl to the fyrste that thou atteny.'
& thenne the fyrst bygonne to pleny,
& sayden that thay hade travayled sore: 550
'These bot on oure hem con streny;
Us thynk us oghe to take more.

47

'"'More haf we served, us thynk so,
That suffred han the dayez hete,
Thenn thyse that wroght not hourez two,
& thou dotz hem us to counterfete.'
Thenne sayde the lorde to on of tho:

X

46

"'The lord acknowledged the limit of day,
and called to his purser: 'Pay these men,
hand out whatever earnings I owe,
and further, so no man finds fault with me,
arrange that they stand in a single row
and pay every person the same: a penny.
Start with the last at the end of the line
and finish with the first who stands at the front.'
But those at the front took offense at that thought,
arguing that they had labored the longest.   550
'These others have only worked for an hour.
More effort should merit greater reward.

47

"''It seems to us we deserve more,
having suffered the heat of the sun all day,
than those who toiled for two hours or less,
yet you offer us earnings of equal amount.'
The master said to one of the men:

'Frende no waning I wyl the yete;
Take that is thyn owne & go.
& I hyred the for a peny agrete,   560
Quy bygynnez thou now to threte?
Watz not a pene thy covenaunt thore?
Fyrre then covenaunde is noght to plete.
Wy schalte thou thenne ask more?

48

""'More wether lawely is me my gyfte
To do wyth myn quat so me lykez?
Other ellez thyn yghe to lyther is lyfte,
For I am goude & non byswykez.'
Thus schal I," quod Kryste, "hit skyfte:
The laste schal be the fyrst that strykez,   570
& the fyrst the laste, be he never so swyft;
For mony ben called, thagh fewe be mykez."
Thus pore men her part ay pykez,
Thagh thay com late & lyttel wore;
&, thagh her sweng wyth lyttel atslykez,
The merci of God is much the more.

49

'More haf I of joye & blysse hereinne,
Of ladyschyp gret & lyvez blom,

'Friend, our deal is not in doubt,
take what I owe you and get off home.
I hired you for a penny, that was our pact,   560
but now you argue at our agreement.
A penny was the price according to our contract.
It is wrong to raise the terms by wrangling,
so what do you mean by asking for more?

48

'"Moreover, can it be a misdemeanor
to do whatever I wish with my wealth?
Do you mean to take advantage of me
because I'm a just and generous man?'
So I practice by the same principle," says Christ:
"The last shall be first to be given their lot   570
and the first and fastest shall be left till last,
for many are called but few are chosen."
Thus the poor shall always have their portion:
though they come late, and in little time
their labor is spent with scant results,
God will be all the more merciful.

49

'I have in this place more peace and bliss,
more status as a lady and fullness of life

570–72. Matthew 20:16: "So shall the last be first, and the first last. For many are
called, but few chosen."

Then alle the wyghez in the worlde myght wynne
By the way of ryght to aske dome.   580
Whether welnygh now I con bygynne,
In eventyde into the vyne I come;
Fyrst of my hyre my Lorde con mynne,
I watz payed anon of al & sum.
Yet other ther werne that toke more tom,
That swange & swat for long yore,
That yet of hyre nothynk thay nom,
Paraunter noght schal toyere more.'

        50

Then more I meled & sayde apert:
'Me thynk thy tale unresounable;   590
Goddez ryght is redy & evermore rert,
Other Holy Wryt is bot a fable;
In Sauter is sayd a verce overte
That spekez a poynt determynable:
"Thou quytez uchon as hys desserte,
Thou hyghe Kyng ay pretermynable."
Now he that stod the long day stable,
& thou to payment com hym byfore,
Thenne the lasse in werke to take more able,
& ever the lenger the lasse the more.'   600

than any person in the world might win
who seeks a just adjudication.   580
I had barely begun my obedience—
I entered the vineyard at evening, as it were—
yet He did not forget to put me first,
paying me all of my wage forthwith.
Others who labor their whole lifetime
and strive, sweat and slog for ever
are left wanting; they wait for their wage
and may well do so for a year or more.'

50

Then I talked again, more tersely this time:
'I cannot agree with your argument.   590
God is a ready and righteous ruler,
or holy scripture is a hollow fable.
In a clear voice, a verse of the Psalter
is proof of an incontrovertible point.
"Supreme Sovereign, seated in judgment,
you repay each man according to merit."
Now, if you should come to receive payment
before him who labored all day long,
then the last to work claim the larger prize,
and the lesser person makes more profit!'   600

593–96. Psalm 61:12–13: "God hath spoken once, these two things have I heard, that power belongeth to God, and mercy to thee, O Lord; for thou wilt render to every man according to his works."

XI

51

'Of more & lasse in Godez ryche,'
That gentyl sayde, 'lys no joparde,
For ther is uch mon payed inlyche,
Whether lyttel other much be hys rewarde,
For the gentyl Cheventayn is no chyche;
Quethersoever he dele nesch other harde,
He lavez hys gyftez as water of dyche,
Other gotez of golf that never charde.
Hys fraunchyse is large that ever dard
To hym that matz in synne rescoghe;   610
No blysse betz fro hem reparde,
For the grace of God is gret inoghe.

52

'Bot now thou motez me for to mate,
That I my peny haf wrang tan here;
Thou sayz that I that com to late
Am not worthy so gret here.
Where wystez thou ever any bourne abate

XI

51

'In God's domain, more and less
have the same meaning,' said that noble maiden,
'for every person is paid equally
despite how much or little they deserve.
The Almighty Master is no miser;
however stern or restrained His dealings
His gifts surge like water from a stream
or rise from depths that never run dry.
His abundance is boundless; to those believers
who reach to Him to be rescued from sin   610
no happiness would He ever withhold,
for the grace of God is great enough for all.

52

'Yet now you argue in order to outwit me,
saying I was paid my penny improperly,
and claim that because I came so late
I remain unworthy of such a reward.
But have you, in your life, ever heard of someone

Ever so holy in hys prayere
That he ne forfeted by sumkyn gate
The mede sumtyme of hevenez clere?   620
& ay the ofter, the alder thay were,
Thay laften ryght & wroghten woghe.
Mercy & grace moste hem then stere,
For the grace of God is gret innoghe.

53

'Bot innoghe of grace hatz innocent;
As sone as thay arn borne, by lyne
In the water of babtem thay dyssente;
Then arne thay boroght into the vyne.
Anon the day, wyth derk endente,
The myght of deth dotz to enclyne;   630
That wroght never wrang er thenne thay wente
The gentyle Lorde thenne payez hys hyne;
Thay dyden hys heste, thay wern thereine;
Why schulde he not her labour alow,
Yes & pay hem at the fyrst fyne,
For the grace of God is gret innoghe?

54

'Inoghe is knawen that mankyn grete
Fyrste watz wroght to blysse parfyt;
Oure forme fader hit con forfete
Thurgh an apple that he upon con byte;   640
Al wer we dampned for that mete

so wholly devout in holy devotion
that he did not forfeit by some fault or other
the reward of radiant heaven he had sought?   620
And the older they grow, the more often
they risk choosing wrong before right,
so must seek mercy many times over
and pray that God has grace enough for all.

53

'But the innocent have enough inherent grace.
After being born they are duly baptized,
immersed at once in holy water,
and so they venture into the vineyard.
Soon their day, edged with darkness,
descends at dusk into deathly nighttime,   630
and the Lord allots His laborers their allowance
who were blameless during their brief lives.
They did as He asked within those acres,
so rightly He rewards them all with their wage.
Yes, pays them first and pays them in full,
for the grace of God is great enough for all.

54

'Enough is known to acknowledge that man
was first formed for a life of perfection,
but our forefather, Adam, forfeited bliss
by tasting the forbidden fruit on his tongue.   640
By eating that apple he damned us all

To dyghe in doel out of delyt,
& sythen wende to helle hete,
Therinne to won wythoute respyt.
Bot ther oncom a bote as-tyt;
Ryche blod ran on rode so roghe,
& wynne water then at that plyt;
The grace of God wex gret innoghe.

55

'Innoghe ther wax out of that welle,
Blod & water of brode wounde: 650
The blod us boght fro bale of helle,
& delyvered us of the deth secounde;
The water is baptem, the sothe to telle,
That folwed the glayve so grymly grounde,
That waschez away the gyltez felle
That Adam wyth inne deth us drounde.
Now is ther noght in the worlde rounde
Bytwene us & blysse bot that he withrow,
& that is restored in sely stounde,
& the grace of God is gret innogh.   660

to die in sorrow, deprived of delight,
then fall to the flaming fires of hell
and be punished without reprieve or escape.
But salvation was ours eventually,
when crimson blood and clear water
dripped on the cruel cross of Christ,
because God's grace was great enough.

55

'From that broad wound, enough bright blood
and holy water welled earthward.   650
The blood released us from relentless hell
and saved us all from a second death.
The water that streamed, it is worth saying,
spilled on the spear which spiked our Lord,
to banish, by baptism, those deadly sins
of Adam's making, in which we were mired.
In a blessed hour He restored our bliss,
and now there is nothing in this wide world
that stands between us and ecstasy,
for the grace of God is great enough.   660

649–56. John 19:34: "But one of the soldiers with a spear opened his side, and immediately there came out blood and water."

XII

56

Grace innogh the mon may have
That synnez thenne newe, yif hym repente,
Bot wyth sorow & syt he mot hit crave,
& byde the payne therto is bent.
Bot resoun of ryght, that con not rave,
Savez evermore the innossent;
Hit is a dom that never God gave,
That ever the gyltlez schulde be schente.
The gyltyf may contryssyoun hente,
& be thurgh mercy to grace thryght;   670
Bot he to gyle that never glente,
As inoscente is saf & ryghte.

57

'Ryght thus I knaw wel in this cas,
Two men to save is god by skylle;
The ryghtwys man schal se hys face,
The harmlez hathel schal com hym tylle.

XII

56

'The man will be granted grace enough
who repeats his sin but solemnly repents,
and seeks out grace with sincere sorrow
and suffers the pains of true penitence.
But judgment and justice go hand in hand,
and will always save the guiltless soul.
God's law would never allow
those pure in thought and deed to be punished.
The guilty must plead for His forgiveness
and through remorse be offered mercy,   670
but those who resist all slyness and deceit
are assured salvation through innocence.

57

'So what I say is right by reason.
God will spare two sorts of people:
the righteous man shall see His face,
and the innocent man shall be called forward.

The Sauter hyt satz thus in a pace:
"Lorde, quo schal klymbe thy hygh hylle,
Other rest wythinne thy holy place?"
Hymself to onsware he is not dylle: 680
"Hondelyngez harme that dyt not ille,
That is of hert bothe clene & lyght,
Ther schal hys step stable stylle;"
The innosent is ay saf by ryght.

58

'The ryghtwys man also sertayn
Aproche he schal that proper pyle
That takez not her lyf in vayne,
Ne glaverez her neghbor wyth no gyle.
Of thys ryghtwys saw Salamon playn,
How kyntly oure Kyng hym con aquyle;   690
By wayez ful streght he con hym strayn,
& scheued hym the rengne of God awhyle,
As quo says: "Lo yon lovely yle!
Thou may hit wynne if thou be wyghte."
Bot hardyly, wythoute peryle,
The innosent is ay save by ryghte.

As the Psalter inquires with the following question:
"Lord, who shall scale your steep summit
and come to rest in your holy realm?"
And the psalmist is prompt to reply to himself: 680
"He who did no harm with his hands,
who harbored no evil or hurt in his heart,
shall find in heaven a firm footing."
By right the innocent are always safe.

58

'And the righteous too will find a route
to the shining citadel, that much is certain:
those who lived without folly or lie,
who were never false with friends or neighbors.
Of the righteous man, Solomon reminds us
how Wisdom obtained honor for him   690
by leading him along the narrow lane
with heaven's kingdom in sight up ahead,
as if to imply, "That lovely isle
is yours to gain if you keep going."
Because undeniably and without a doubt
the innocent reach there, as of right.

678. Psalm 14:1–3: "Lord, who shall dwell in thy tabernacle? or who shall rest in thy holy hill? He that walketh without blemish, and worketh justice: He that speaketh truth in his heart, who hath not used deceit in his tongue: Nor hath done evil to his neighbour: nor taken up a reproach against his neighbours."
689–94. Wisdom 10:10: " She conducted the just, when he fled from his brother's wrath, through the right ways, and shewed him the kingdom of God, and gave him the knowledge of the holy things, made him honourable in his labours, and accomplished his labours."

59

'Anende ryghtwys men yet saytz a gome—
David in Sauter, if ever ye saw hit:
"Lorde, thy servaunt draw never to dome,
For non lyvande to the is justyfyet."   700
Forthy to corte quen thou schal com,
Ther alle oure causez schal be tryed,
Alegge the ryght thou may be innome
By thys ilke spech I have asspyed.
Bot he on rode that blody dyed,
Delfully thurgh hondez thryght,
Gyve the to passe, when thou arte tryed,
By innocens & not by ryghte.

60

'Ryghtwysly quo con rede,
He loke on bok & be awayed   710
How Jesus hym welke in arethede,
& burnez her barnez unto hym brayde.
For happe & hele that fro hym yede
To touch her chylder thay fayr hym prayed.
His dessypelez wyth blame let be hem bede,

59

'Although, with regard to righteous men,
read what David wrote in the Psalter:
"Lord, never summon your servant to judgment,
for not one person is worthy in your presence."   700
So when you come before the court
where cases are called and heard in due course,
even the righteous might be refused,
for reasons recorded in those writings.
But may Christ who died on the cruel cross,
horribly pierced through His pale hands,
set you free in that final trial,
if not by right then by innocence.

60

'You who righteously read the bible,
remember this parable and heed its instruction: 710
when Jesus passed among His people
they brought their babes and bairns toward Him
and humbly begged Him to hold their offspring,
hoping for a touch of His happiness and health.
His disciples lectured them: "Leave Him alone,"

699–700. Psalm 142:2: "And enter not into judgment with thy servant: for in thy
sight no man living shall be justified."

711–24. Luke 18:15–17: "And they brought unto him also infants, that he might
touch them. Which when the disciples saw, they rebuked them. But Jesus, call-
ing them together, said: Suffer children to come to me, and forbid them not: for
of such is the kingdom of God. Amen, I say to you: Whosoever shall not receive
the kingdom of God as a child, shall not enter into it."

& wyth her resounez ful fele restayed.
Jesus thenne hem swetely sayde:
"Do way, let chylder unto me tyght;
To suche is hevenryche arayed";
The innocent is ay saf by ryght.   720

and warned the crowd with discouraging words.
Then Jesus spoke, saying to them gently,
"Allow the little ones to come to their Lord,
heaven is always ready to receive them."
So rightly the innocent shall always be saved.   720

XIII

61

Jesus con calle to hym hys mylde,
& sayde hys ryche no wyz myght wynne
Bot he com thyder ryght as a chylde,
Other ellez never more com therinne.
Harmlez, truwe, & vndefylde,
Wythouten mote other mascle of sulpande synne—
Quen such ther cnoken on the bylde,
Tyt schal hem men the yate unpynne.
Ther is the blys that con not blynne
That the jueler soghte thurgh perre pres,   730
& solde alle hys goud, bothe wolen & lynne,
To bye hym a perle watz mascellez.

XIII

61

'Christ then called His dutiful disciples
to remind them none had the right to His realm
unless they approached with the purity of children,
otherwise they had no hope of entering.
Faultless, honest and undefiled,
not stained or shamed by corrupting sin:
when the innocent knock and ask to come in
the bolts of the gate shall be drawn back.
And unending kinds of joy in that kingdom
the jeweler pursues through his precious stone,   730
selling linen and wool—his life's work—
to purchase an incomparable pearl.

729–39. Matthew 13:45–46: "Again, the kingdom of heaven is like to a merchant
seeking good pearls, who, when he had found one pearl of great price, went his
way, and sold all that he had, and bought it."

62

'"This maskellez perle, that boght is dere,
The joueler gef fore alle hys god,
Is lyke the reme of hevenesse clere";
So sayde the Fader of folde & flode;
For hit is wemlez, clene, & clere,
& endelez rounde, & blythe of mode,
& commune to alle that ryghtwys were.
Lo, even in myddez my breste hit stode!   740
My Lorde the Lombe, that schede hys blode,
He pyght hit there in token of pes.
I rede the forsake the worlde wode,
& porchace thy perle maskelles.'

63

'O maskelez perle in perlez pure,
That berez,' quod I, 'the perle of prys,
Quo formed the thy fayre fygure?
That wroght thy wede, he watz ful wys.
Thy beaute com never of nature;
Pymalyon paynted never thy vys,   750
Ne Arystotel nawther by hys lettrure
Of carpe the kynde these propertyz.
Thy colour passez the flour-de-lys;
Thyn angel-hauyng so clene cortez—
Breve me, bryght; quat kyn offys
Berez the perle so maskellez?'

62

'This costly, incomparable pearl,
for which the jeweler will sell his stock,
is like the luminous empire of heaven—
so says the Lord of land and seas.
Flawless, fathomless, clean and clear,
a sublime circle and endless sphere
that belongs jointly to the just. It sits
burnished and bright at the center of my breast.   740
My Lord the Lamb, who shed his blood,
set it there as a symbol of peace.
I suggest you forsake this insane world
and purchase your incomparable pearl.'

63

'Oh pure and incomparable pearl,
bearer of the priceless pearl,' I said,
'whoever fashioned your fine features
and wove what you wear is a miracle worker.
Your beauty was never derived from nature.
Pygmalion failed to paint such a face,   750
and not for all his letters and lectures
could Aristotle tell of your attributes.
Your pallor and complexion surpasses the lily,
from every angle you are angel-like.
Exquisite being, describe the position
you command as an incomparable pearl.'

64

'My maskelez Lambe that al may bete,'
Quod scho, 'my dere Destyne,
Me ches to hys make althagh unmete;
Sumtyme semed that assemble,   760
When I wente fro yor worlde wete.
He calde me to hys bonerte:
"Cum hyder to me, my lemman swete,
For mote ne spot is non in the."
He gef me myght & als bewte;
In hys blod he wesch my wede on dese,
& coronde clene in vergynte,
& pyght me in perlez maskellez.'

65

'Why maskellez bryd, that bryght con flambe,
That reiatez hatz so ryche & ryf,   770
Quat kyn thyng may be that Lambe
That the wolde wedde unto hys wyf?
Over alle other so hygh thou clambe
To lede wyth hym so ladyly lyf?
So mony a comly onunder cambe

64

'My peerless, incomparable Lamb,'
she declared, 'my dearest destiny and Lord;
He beckoned me to become His bride,
a match that many might find unfitting.   760
When I departed your dismal world
He brought me toward His blessedness.
"Come to me now, my beloved," He called.
"There is no blame or blemish in your being."
He bestowed both strength and beauty on me,
washed and cleansed my clothes in His blood,
then crowned me a pure and virgin queen
and cast me in incomparable pearls.'

65

'Bright and incomparable bride,
who enjoys such royal rank,' I replied,   770
'what kind of lord or king is that Lamb
to want to wed you as His wife?
You scrambled and clambered and scaled the heights
to sit at His side and be called His queen.
Many beautiful women have slogged and slaved

764. Song of Solomon 4:7: "Thou art all fair, O my love, and there is not a spot in thee."
768. Isaiah 61:10: "I will greatly rejoice in the Lord, and my soul shall be joyful in my God: for he hath clothed me with the garments of salvation: and with the robe of justice he hath covered me, as a bridegroom decked with a crown, and as a bride adorned with her jewels."

For Kryst han lyved in much stryf;
& thou con alle tho dere outdryf,
& fro that maryag al other depres,
Al only thyself so stout & styf,
A makelez may & maskellez.'   780

and suffered strife in the name of our Saviour,
yet you brushed all rival brides aside,
and chased away challengers to that marriage.
You alone had the stamina and strength,
impressive and incomparable pearl.'   780

XIV

66

'Maskelles,' quod that myry quene,
'Unblemyst I am, wythouten blot,
& that may I wyth mensk menteene;
Bot "makelez quene" thenne sayde I not.
The Lambes wyves in blysse we bene,
A hondred & forty thowsande flot,
As in the Apocalyppez hit is sene;
Sant John hem saw al in a knot
On the hyl of Syon, that semly clot;
The apostel hem segh in gostly drem   790
Arayed to the weddyng in that hyl-coppe,
The newe cyte o Jerusalem.

XIV

66

That incomparable pearl then spoke.
'I am unblemished and without blame,
honours I hold with my head held high.
But "incomparable" I never implied.
The brides who live with our Lord in bliss
are a hundred and forty four thousand strong,
as is written in the Book of Revelation.
Saint John saw them gathered together
on the hill of Sion, that sacred knoll,
and in the apostle's dream they were dressed   790
for their wedding ceremony there on that summit,
in the city of new Jerusalem.

783–86. Revelation 14:3: "And they sung as it were a new canticle, before the throne, and before the four living creatures, and the ancients; and no man could say the canticle, but those hundred forty-four thousand, who were purchased from the earth."

791f. Revelation 19:7–8: "Let us be glad and rejoice, and give glory to him; for the marriage of the Lamb is come, and his wife hath prepared herself. And it is granted to her that she should clothe herself with fine linen, glittering and white. For the fine linen is the justification of saints."

67

'Of Jerusalem I in speche spelle.
If thou wyl knaw what kyn he be—
My Lombe, my Lorde, my dere Juelle,
My Joy, my Blys, my Lemman fre—
The profete Ysaye of hym con melle
Pitously of hys debonerte:
"That gloryous Gyltlez that mon con quelle,
Wythouten any sake of felonye,   800
As a schep to the slaght ther lad watz he;
&, as lombe that clypper in lande nem,
So closed he hys mouth fro uch query,
Quen Juez hym jugged in Jerusalem."

68

'In Jerusalem watz my Lemman slayn,
& rent on rode wyth boyez bolde;
Al oure balez to bere ful bayn,
He toke on hymself oure carez colde;

67

'Telling the tale of Jerusalem
sheds light on what our Lord is like,
my Lamb, my blessed and beloved one,
my joy, my bliss, my precious jewel.
The compassionate prophet Isaiah in his sermon
was moved to speak of His mild manner:
"That glorious, guiltless man was killed,
nailed to a cross with no crime to His name.   800
He was led to the slaughter like a sheep.
And like the lamb in the shearer's hands
He suffered the blades of blame in silence
when judged by the Jews in Jerusalem."

68

'In Jerusalem my love was slain,
His flesh pierced by pitiless yobs.
Always willing to shoulder our woes
He bore our crimes on His broad back.

797–803. Isaiah 53:3–8: "Despised, and the most abject of men, a man of sorrows,
and acquainted with infirmity: and his look was as it were hidden and despised,
whereupon we esteemed him not. Surely he hath borne our infirmities and car-
ried our sorrows: and we have thought him as it were a leper, and as one struck
by God and afflicted. But he was wounded for our iniquities, he was bruised for
our sins: the chastisement of our peace was upon him, and by his bruises we are
healed . . . He was offered because it was his own will, and he opened not his
mouth: he shall be led as a sheep to the slaughter, and shall be dumb as a lamb
before his shearer, and he shall not open his mouth. He was taken away from
distress, and from judgment: who shall declare his generation?"

Wyth boffetez watz hys face flayn,
That watz so fayr on to byholde;   810
For synne he set hymself in vayn,
That never hade non hymself to wolde;
For us he lette hym flyghe & folde
& brede upon a bostwys bem,
As meke as lomb that no playnt tolde;
For us he swalt in Jerusalem.

69

'Jerusalem, Jordan & Galalye,
Ther as baptysed the goude Saynt Jon,
His wordez acorded to Ysaye.
When Jesus con to hym warde gon,   820
He sayde of hym thys professye:
"Lo Godez Lombe as truwe as ston,
That dotz away the synnez dryghe
That alle thys worlde hatz wroght upon!
Hymself ne wroght never yet non,

Brutal assaults and bitter blows
left His beautiful features bloodied and bruised.   810
For sinners He set His innocence aside
though He Himself had never sinned.
For us He was tortured, twisted and torn
then stretched and broken across a beam.
Compliant and uncomplaining as a lamb
He laid down His life in Jerusalem.

69

'Jerusalem, Jordan and Galilee
were the places where John the Baptist preached,
and his words agree with those of Isaiah.
As Jesus walked to where John was standing   820
the prophet made the following remark:
"The lamb of God is a steadfast stone,
a solid rock to resist all wrong
and bear the weight of the world's sins.
Christ Himself committed no crime

809–16. Matthew 26:67: "Then did they spit in his face, and buffeted him: and others struck his face with the palms of their hands."

817–18. Matthew 3:13: "Then cometh Jesus from Galilee to the Jordan, unto John, to be baptized by him."

819–24. John 1:29: "The next day, John saw Jesus coming to him, and he saith: Behold the Lamb of God, behold him who taketh away the sin of the world."

823–26. Isaiah 53:6, 9, 11: "All we like sheep have gone astray, every one hath turned aside into his own way: and the Lord hath laid on him the iniquity of us all . . . And he shall give the ungodly for his burial, and the rich for his death: because he hath done no iniquity, neither was there deceit in his mouth . . . Because his soul hath laboured, he shall see and be filled: by his knowledge shall this my just servant justify many, and he shall bear their iniquities."

Whether on hymself he con al clem.
Hys generacyoun quo recen con,
That dyghed for us in Jerusalem?"

70

'In Jerusalem thus my Lemman swete
Twyez for lombe watz taken there,   830
By truwe recorde of ayther prophete,
For mode so meke & al hys fare;
The thryde tyme is therto ful mete
In Apokalypez wryten ful yare.
In mydez the trone, there sayntez sete,
The apostel John hym saw as bare,
Lesande the boke with levez sware
There seven syngnettez wern sette inseme;
& at that syght uche douth con dare,
In helle, in erthe, & Jerusalem.   840

but owned the blame on our behalf.
Who can account for his ancestry?
He died for us in Jerusalem."

70

'In Jerusalem, then, my beloved Lord
was twice depicted as a Lamb   830
in the true chronicles of the two prophets
because of His meek and mild demeanor.
And a third example agrees thoroughly,
as written clearly in Revelation.
Around the throne where saints thronged
the apostle John saw the Lord Jesus
clearly opening the covers of a book
with square leaves and seven seals.
Each company, seeing that sight, bowed down,
on earth, in hell and Jerusalem.   840

827. Isaiah 53:8: "He was taken away from distress, and from judgment: who shall declare his generation? because he is cut off out of the land of the living: for the wickedness of my people have I struck him."
835–40. Revelation 5:1, 3, 7–8: "And I saw in the right hand of him that sat on the throne, a book written within and without, sealed with seven seals . . . And no man was able, neither in heaven, nor on earth, nor under the earth, to open the book, nor to look on it . . . And he came and took the book out of the right hand of him that sat on the throne. And when he had opened the book, the four living creatures, and the four and twenty ancients fell down before the Lamb, having every one of them harps, and golden vials full of odours, which are the prayers of saints."

XV

71

Thys Jerusalem Lombe hade never pechche
Of other huee bot quyt jolyf,
That mot ne masklle moght on streche,
For wolle quyte so ronk & ryf.
Forthy uche saule that hade never teche,
Is to that Lombe a worthyly wyf;
&, thagh uch day a store he feche,
Among us commez non other strot ne stryf,
Bot uchon enle we wolde were fyf;
The mo the myryer, so God me blesse.   850
In compayny gret our luf con thryf
In honour more & never the lesse.

72

'Lasse of blysse may non us bryng,
That beren thys perle upon oure bereste,

XV

71

'That immaculate Lamb of Jerusalem
was whiter than white, covered in wool
so brilliantly bright no blot or stain
could cling to the coat and discolor the fleece.
So every soul untainted by sin
is a worthy wife to Christ our Lord,
and no matter how many He welcomes in
no tension or bitterness exists between us.
In fact, let five times the number follow—
the more the merrier, so bless me God.   850
Among our exalted community
our love becomes more and never less.

72

'No one can lessen the blissful life
of those who bear the pearl on their breast;

841–44. 1 Peter 1:19: "But with the precious blood of Christ, as of a lamb unspot-
ted and undefiled,"

For thay of mote couthe never mynge
Of spotlez perlez that beren the creste.
Althagh oure corses in clottez clynge,
& ye remen for rauthe wythouten reste,
We thurghoutly haven cnawyng;
Of on dethe ful oure hope is drest;   860
The lombe us gladez, oure care is kest;
He myrthez us alle at uch a mes;
Uchonez blysse is breme & beste,
& never onez honour yet never the les.

73

'Lest les thou leve my tale farande,
In Appocalyppece is wryten in wro:
"I seghe," says John, "the Loumbe hym stande
On the mount of Syon ful thryven & thro,
& wyth hym maydennez an hundrethe thowsande
& fowre & forty thowsande mo.   870
On alle her forhedez wryten I fande
The Lombez nome, hys Faderez also.
A hue fro heven I herde thoo,

we who are crowned with the flawless crest
are incapable of feud or fight.
And though our corpses decay in the clay
and you cry with lament unremittingly,
one hope above all stays alive in our hearts,
that our souls are saved by a single death.   860
The Lamb releases us from despair;
guests at His table, we give our thanks
for He offers intense joy to us all
and no one's honor is ever made less.

73

'Nevertheless, if you think me a liar,
recall what these verses from Revelation reveal:
"I saw," said Saint John, "on Sion's summit
the Lamb of God in all His grandeur,
with a host of a hundred thousand virgins
and forty four thousand more at His side.   870
And the letters of the name of the Lamb were written
across their foreheads, and His father's name too.
Then out of the heavens I heard a shout

860. Hebrews 10:14: "For by one oblation he hath perfected for ever them that
are sanctified."
866–900. Revelation 14:1–3: "And I beheld, and lo a lamb stood upon mount
Sion, and with him an hundred forty-four thousand, having his name, and the
name of his Father, written on their foreheads. And I heard a voice from heaven,
as the noise of many waters, and as the voice of great thunder; and the voice
which I heard, was as the voice of harpers, harping on their harps. And they
sung as it were a new canticle, before the throne, and before the four living crea-
tures, and the ancients; and no man could say the canticle, but those hundred
forty-four thousand, who were purchased from the earth."

Lyk flodez fele laden, runnen on resse;
&, as thunder throwez in torrez blo,
That lote, I leve, watz never the les.

74

'"Nautheles, thagh hit schowted scharpe,
& ledden loude althagh hit were,
A note ful newe I herde hem warpe;
To lysten that watz ful lufly dere.   880
As harporez harpen in her harpe,
That newe songe thay songen ful cler;
In sounande notez a gentyl carpe,
Ful fayre the modez thay fonge in fere.
Ryght byfore Godez chayere,
& the fowre bestez that hym obes,
& the aldermen so sadde of chere,
Her songe thay songen never the les.

75

'"Nowthelese non watz never so quoynt,
For alle the craftez that ever thay knewe,   890
That of that songe myght synge a poynt,
Bot that meyny the Lombe that suwe,
For thay arn boght fro the urthe aloynte

like the roar of many rivers in flood,
or thunder cannoning through black clouds—
such a sound, I believe, and nothing less.

74

'"As relentlessly as that cry rang out
reverberating with vibrant voices,
within that chorus came newer notes,
pleasant to hear, peaceful on the ear.   880
Like harpists strumming their stringed harps
the sound of that song was sweet and clear,
a melody of mellifluous words
with harmonies that would melt the heart.
There in front of the throne of God
and the four obedient beasts at His feet
and the aldermen with austere faces
the singers were singing ceaselessly.

75

'"Nevertheless, no singer ever known,
no matter how able or practiced in their art,   890
could perform a single refrain of that song,
except the chosen ones of His choir.
Distant from earth, they are all redeemed,

---

886. Ezekiel 1:10: "And as for the likeness of their faces: there was the face of a
man, and the face of a lion on the right side of all the four: and the face of an ox,
on the left side of all the four: and the face of an eagle over all the four."

As newe fryt to God ful due,
& to the gentyl Lombe hit arn anioynt,
As lyk to hymself of lote & huwe;
For never lesyng ne tale untruwe
Ne towched her tonge for no dysstresse."
That moteles meyny may never remuwe
Fro that maskelez Mayster never the les.'   900

76

'Nevertheles let be my thonc,'
Quod I. 'My perle, thagh I appose,
I schulde not tempte thy wyt so wlonc,
To Krystez chambre that art ichose.
I am bot mokke & mul among,
& thou so ryche a reken rose,
& bydez here by thys blysful bonc
Ther lyvez lyste may never lose.
Now hynde that sympelnesse conez enclose,
I wolde the aske a thynge expresse;   910
&, thagh I be bustwys as a blose,
Let my bone vayl neverthelese.

since the first of the fruit to fall shall be God's.
Clean like Him in character and speech
they unite with their noble Lord at the last,
for no falsehood or untrue tale
ever tainted their tongues, whatever their troubles.
Nothing could part heaven's spotless household
from their flawless Lord, or lessen their bond."'   900

76

'Lady, never think any less of my thanks,'
I said, 'if I keep on questioning my pearl.
I am not worthy of challenging the wisdom
of a bride chosen for Christ's chamber,
nothing but a mix of dust and muck,
and you such a rare and regal rose,
abiding here on this beautiful bank
where life's fruitfulness never fades.
But from you, sincerity itself, I seek
an honest answer to what I ask.   910
I may be a crude and uncultured man,
nevertheless let my question stand.

XVI

77

'Neverthelese cler I yow bycalle,
If ye con se hyt be to done;
As thou art gloryous wythouten galle,
Wythnay thou never my ruful bone.
Haf ye no wonez in castel-walle,
Ne maner ther ye may mete & won?
Thou tellez me of Jerusalem the ryche ryalle,
Ther David dere watz dyght on trone,   920
Bot by thyse holtez hit con not hone,
Bot in Judee hit is, that noble note.
As ye ar maskelez under mone,
Your wonez schulde be wythouten mote.

78

'Thys motelez meyny thou conez of mele,
Of thousandez thryght so gret a route,
A gret cete, for ye arn fele,
Yow byhod have, wythouten doute;
So cumly a pakke of joly juele,

XVI

77

'So unless you object, beautiful lady,
I call upon you, most courteously,
as a person untouched by impurity,
and pray my appeal will prompt a reply.
Have you no castle, enclosed by walls,
or manor house with meeting halls?
You speak of Jerusalem's sovereign lands
where David ruled with great dignity,   920
but Jerusalem is in Judea
and not to be found in these forests nearby.
Faultless underneath heaven, you deserve
a fitting palace, equally flawless.

78

'For this company of flawless creatures you describe,
a great throng, thousands strong,
there must exist a magnificent city
to house you all and hold you safe.
How unjust if such splendid jewels

Wer evel don schulde lygh theroute.   930
& by thyse bonkez ther I con gele
& I se no bygyng nawhere aboute,
I trowe alone ye lenge & loute
To loke on the glory of thys gracious gote.
If thou hatz other bygyngez stoute,
Now tech me to that myry mote.'

79

'That mote thou menez in Judy londe,'
That specyal spyce then to me spakk,
'That is the cyte that the Lombe con fonde
To soffer inne sor for manez sake—   940
The olde Jerusalem to understonde;
For there the olde gulte watz don to slake.
Bot the newe, that lyght of Godez sonde,
The apostel in Apocalyppce in theme con take.
The Lombe ther wythouten spottez blake
Hatz feryed thyder hys fayre flote;
&, as hys flok is wythouten flake,
So is hys mote wythouten moote.

80

'Of motes two to carpe clene,
& Jerusalem hyght bothe nawtheles,   950
That nys to yow no more to mene
Bot cete of God, other syght of pes:
In that on oure pes watz mad at ene,

slept rough in the world without a roof,   930
yet the length and breadth of this riverbank
I see no buildings anywhere about.
You stroll here alone alongside this stream
and gaze at the gracefully running waters,
but where do you stay? If a citadel stands,
let me follow you to that flawless place.'

79

That flawless figure then said to me:
'The city you speak of in the land of Judea
is the same city the Lord sought out
in which to suffer the sins of mankind.   940
In other words, old Jerusalem,
where Christ atoned for Adam's crime.
But new Jerusalem, set to ground by God,
the apostle writes of in Revelation;
there the Lamb, unblemished by blackness,
guided His fair and favorite people.
And because that company is clean of heart,
so the city is flawless and without fault.

80

'To speak without flaw of those two cities,
both known by the name Jerusalem,   950
a term which to you means little more
than "City of God," or "Vision of Peace"—
in one our reconciliation was secured

Wyth payne to suffer the Lombe hit chese;
In that other is noght bot pes to glene
That ay schal laste wythouten reles.
That is the borgh that we to pres
Fro that oure flesch be layd to rote;
Ther glory & blysse schal ever encres
To the meyny that is wythouten mote.'   960

81

'Motelez may so meke & mylde,'
Then sayde I to that lufly flor,
'Bryng me to that bygly bylde,
& let me se thy blysful bor.'
That schene sayde: 'That God wyl schylde;
Thou may not enter wythinne hys tor,
Bot of the Lombe I have the aquylde
For a syght therof thurgh gret favor.
Utwyth to se that clene cloystor
Thou may, bot inwyth not a fote;   970
To strech in the strete thou hatz no vygour
Bot thou wer clene wythouten mote.

when the Lamb chose to suffer pain in that place;
in the other there is only infinite peace,
a haven where happiness lasts for ever,
a heavenly home we speedily head for
when our flesh and bones turn foul in the grave.
There glory and bliss will grow for those
who are residents of that flawless realm.'   960

81

'Flawless girl, guileless and gentle,'
I said to that fresh and radiant flower,
'show me the way to that shining castle,
lead me to the house you call your home.'
But she firmly refused. 'God forbids it.
You cannot enter His holy estate.
By the grace of the Lamb I have gained permission
for you to stand in sight of that city
and glimpse its glory from beyond the gate.
But you must not set one foot inside.   970
You have no right to stride through its streets
unless you are flawless and free of fault.

XVII

82

'If I this mote the schal unhyde,
Bow up towarde thys bornez heved,
& I anendez the on this syde
Schal suwe, tyl thou to a hil be veved.'
Then wolde I no lenger byde,
Bot lurked by launcez so lufly leved,
Tyl on a hyl that I asspyed
& blusched on the burghe, as I forth dreved,   980

XVII

82

'To find a view of that flawless place
walk upstream alongside the water
to the valley head, till you come to a hill,
and I will follow on this far bank.'
Then I wouldn't delay a moment longer,
but went beneath leaves through dappled light
till I saw that city perched on its summit,
and stumbled toward that stunning sight   980

973–1032. Revelation 21:10–21: "And he took me up in spirit to a great and high mountain: and he shewed me the holy city Jerusalem coming down out of heaven from God, having the glory of God, and the light thereof was like to a precious stone, as to the jasper stone, even as crystal. And it had a wall great and high, having twelve gates, and in the gates twelve angels, and names written thereon, which are the names of the twelve tribes of the children of Israel. On the east, three gates: and on the north, three gates: and on the south, three gates: and on the west, three gates. And the wall of the city had twelve foundations, and in them, the twelve names of the twelve apostles of the Lamb. And he that spoke with me, had a measure of a reed of gold, to measure the city and the gates thereof, and the wall. And the city lieth in a foursquare, and the length thereof is as great as the breadth: and he measured the city with the golden reed for twelve thousand furlongs, and the length and the height and the breadth thereof are equal. And he measured the wall thereof an hundred and forty-four cubits, the measure of a man, which is of an angel. And the building of the wall

Beyonde the brok fro me warde breved,
That schyrrer then sunne wyth schaftez schon.
In the Apokalypce is the fasoun preved,
As devysez hit the apostel John.

83

As John the apostel hit saw wyth syght,
I syghe that cyty of gret renoun,
Jerusalem so newe & ryally dyght,
As hit watz lyght fro the heven adoun.
The borgh watz al of brende golde bryght,
As glemande glas burnist broun,   990
Wyth gentyl gemmez anunder pyght;
Wyth bantelez twelve on basyng boun,
The foundementez twelve of riche tenoun;
Uch tabelment watz a serlypez ston;
As derely devysez this ilk toun
In Apocalyppez the apostel John.

some distance away beyond the brook,
shining brighter than the sun's beams,
in its features, facets, size and structure
just as Saint John revealed in Revelation.

83

Yes just as the apostle John described it
I saw for myself that exalted city:
the new Jerusalem, luminously rich,
as though descended from heaven's heights.
Its buildings gleamed with pure gold,
blazing and glinting like burnished glass.   990
They stood on a base of precious stones
formed of twelve well-fastened tiers,
a firm and cleverly fashioned foundation,
each stratum cut from a seamless gem,
as in the writings of Revelation
where John the apostle depicts the apocalypse.

---

thereof was of jasper stone: but the city itself pure gold, like to clear glass. And
the foundations of the wall of the city were adorned with all manner of pre-
cious stones. The first foundation was jasper: the second, sapphire: the third, a
chalcedony: the fourth, an emerald: the fifth, sardonyx: the sixth, sardius: the
seventh, chrysolite: the eighth, beryl: the ninth, a topaz: the tenth, a chrysopra-
sus: the eleventh, a jacinth: the twelfth, an amethyst. And the twelve gates are
twelve pearls, one to each: and every several gate was of one several pearl. And
the street of the city was pure gold, as it were transparent glass."

84

As John thise stonez in writ con nemme,
I knew the name after his tale:
Jasper hyght the fyrst gemme
That I on the fyrst basse con wale;   1000
He glente grene in the lowest hemme;
Saffer helde the secounde stale;
The calsydoyne thenne wythouten wemme
In the thryd table con purly pale;
The emerade the furthe so grene of scale;
The sardonyse the fyfthe ston;
The sexte the rybe he con hit wale
In the Apocalyppce the apostel John.

85

Yet joyned John the crysolyt,
The seventhe gemme in fundament;   1010
The aghtthe the beryl cler & quyt;
The topasye twynne-hew the nente endent;
The crysopase the tenthe is tyght;
The jacyngh the enleventhe gent;
The twelfthe, the gentyleste in uch a plyt,
The amatyst purpre wyth ynde blente;
The wal abof the bantels bent
O jasporye, as glas that glysnande schon;
I knew hit by his devysement
In the Apocalyppez, the apostel John.   1020

84

John had described those stones in his scriptures
so I knew their names and also their nature.
I judged the first of those jewels to be jasper,
found at the very bottom of the base,   1000
gleaming green on the lowest layer.
Sapphire occupied the second stage,
and clear, crystalline chalcedony
shone pure and pale on the third plane.
Emerald was fourth with its glaring green finish,
and finely striated sardonyx the fifth,
and ruby the sixth, exactly as stated
by John the apostle when depicting the apocalypse.

85

John also described the chrysolite,
the stone which formed the seventh stage.   1010
The eighth was of brilliantly white beryl,
a table of twin-toned topaz the ninth,
a course of chysoprase the tenth,
noble and elegant jacinth the eleventh,
and twelfth, most trusted in times of trouble,
was a plane of purple and indigo amethyst.
The wall above that tiered base
was jasper, glistening and glittering like glass,
a vision I knew very well from the version
in John the apostle's apocalyptic scriptures.   1020

86

As John devysed yet saw I thare.
Thise twelve degres wern brode & stayre;
The cyte stod abof ful sware,
As longe as brode as hyghe ful fayre—
The stretez of golde as glasse al bare,
The wal of jasper that glent as glayre;
The wonez wythinne enurned ware
Wyth alle kynnez perre that moght repayre.
Thenne helde uch sware of this manayre,
Twelve forlonge space er ever hit fon,   1030
Of heght, of brede, of lenthe, to cayre,
For meten hit saw the apostel John.

86

Then I saw still more of what John described:
those twelve tiers were broad and steep
with the city on top, perfectly square,
equal in every dimension, and exquisite.
The golden streets sparkled like glass,
and jasper glared as if glazed with egg white.
Inside, those walls were studded and set
with every possible precious stone,
and every square side of that estate
in every dimension measured twelve furlongs,   1030
in height and width and length the same size,
just as John the apostle had judged.

XVIII

87

As John hym wrytez yet more I syghe:
Uch pane of that place had thre yates,
So twelve in pourseut I con asspye,
The portalez pyked of rych platez,
& uch yate of a margyrye,
A parfyt perle that never fatez.
Uchon in scrypture a name con plye
Of Israel barnez, folewande her datez,   1040
That is to say, as her byrth whatez;
The aldest ay fyrst theron watz done.
Such lyght ther lemed in alle the stratez
Hem nedde nawther sunne ne mone.

88

Of sunne ne mone had thay no nede;
The self God watz her lompelyght,
The Lombe her lantyrne wythouten drede;
Thurgh hym blysned the borgh al bryght.
Thurgh woghe & won my lokyng yede,

XVIII

87

And I saw still more of what John had scripted:
each of its aspects had three entrances,
so twelve gates in total were visible.
The portals were plated in expensive metals,
and the doors adorned with a singular pearl,
a perfect pearl that could never fade.
Over every arch in carved characters
the names of the Children of Israel were inscribed   1040
in order of age, that is to say
beginning with the firstborn, and so on and so forth.
Such light illuminated the city's streets
that neither sun nor moon were needed.

88

They needed neither sun nor moon
since God Himself was their guiding light
and the Lamb their lantern. There was no doubt:
through God's brilliance the city glowed.
And all was transparent, so my gaze passed

For sotyle cler noght lette no lyght.   1050
The hyghe trone ther moght ye hede
Wyth alle the apparaylmente umbepyghte,
As John the appostel in termez tyghte;
The hyghe Godez self hit set upone.
A rever of the trone ther ran outryghte
Watz bryghter then bothe the sunne & mone.

89

Sunne ne mone schon never so swete
As that foysoun flode out of that flet;
Swythe hit swange thurgh uch a strete
Wythouten fylthe other galle other glet.   1060
Kyrk therinne watz non yete,
Chapel ne temple that ever watz set;
The Almyghty watz her mynyster mete,
The Lombe the sakerfyse ther to refet.
The yates stoken watz never yet,
Bot evermore open at uche a lone;
Ther entrez non to take reset
That berez any spot anunder mone.

90

The mone may therof acroche no myghte;
To spotty ho is, of body to grym;   1070
& also ther ne is never nyght.
What schulde the mone ther compas clym,
& to-even wyth that worthly lyght

through wall and structure without obstruction,   1050
till I saw with my eyes the high throne
arrayed in awesome ornaments,
as John the apostle correctly recorded,
with God taking His place upon it.
And running directly out of that throne
was a river more radiant than sun and moon.

89

No sun or moon ever shone so sweetly
as the plentiful water that poured through those precincts;
it surged swiftly along every street
without sediment or slime or foaming filth.   1060
No church or chapel had ever been built
or temple constructed within the walls;
God Almighty was their one minster,
the sacrificial Lamb their spiritual food.
The gates were never bolted or barred
but open at every possible approach,
though none may enter in search of sanctuary
who bears any blemish beneath the moon.

90

The moon cannot practice her powers in that place,
she is pockmarked and pitted and impure in person.   1070
Added to which, it is never nighttime.
How could the moon, casting her moonbeams
from celestial circuits, hope to compete

That schynez upon the brokez brym?
The planetez arn in to pouer a plyght,
& the self sunne ful fer to dym.
Aboute that water arn tres ful schym,
That twelve frytez of lyf con bere ful sone;
Twelve sythez on yer thay beren ful frym,
& renowlez newe in uche a mone.   1080

91

Anunder mone so gret mervayle
No fleschly hert ne myght endeure,
As quen I blusched upon that bayly,
So ferly therof watz the fasure.
I stod as stylle as dased quayle
For ferly of that freuch fygure,
That felde I nawther reste ne travayle,
So watz I ravyste wyth glymme pure.
For I dar say wyth conciens sure,
Hade bodyly burne abiden that bone,   1090
Thagh alle clerkez hym hade in cure,
His lyf wer loste anunder mone.

with the light that sheens off that stream's surface?
The planets are pitifully poor in comparison
and the sun too dim by some distance.
The riverbanks were bordered by bright trees
which bore on their boughs the twelve fruits of life;
twelve times a year those trees offer harvest,
their riches returning monthly like the moon.   1080

91

No more amazement under the moon
has a human heart ever had to endure
than when I witnessed the walled city
and marveled at its fabulous feats of form.
I stood as still as a stunned quail,
hypnotized by that holy vision,
every nerve and sense in my body numbed,
enraptured by unrivaled radiance.
And this I declare with a clear conviction:
any mortal man, having seen such a miracle,   1090
despite the craft and cures of his doctor,
would go to his grave beneath the moon.

1077–80. Revelation 22:2: "In the midst of the street thereof, and on both sides of the river, was the tree of life, bearing twelve fruits, yielding its fruits every month, and the leaves of the tree were for the healing of the nations."

XIX

92

Ryght as the maynful mone con rys
Er thenne the day-glem dryve al doun,
So sodanly on a wonder wyse
I watz war of a prosessyoun.
This noble cite of ryche enpryse
Watz sodanly ful wythouten sommoun
Of such vergynez in the same gyse
That watz my blysful anunder croun;   1100
& coronde wern alle of the same fasoun,
Depaynt in perlez & wedez qwyte;
In uchonez breste watz bounden boun
The blysful perle wyth gret delyt.

XIX

92

At the moment the moon began to climb,
before the final setting of the sun,
I became aware in a wonderful way
of the sudden presence of a long procession.
The streets of that famous and fabled city
were all at once and without warning
streaming with virgins in the very clothing
my dearest beloved was dressed in herself.   1100
They were similarly crowned in the same manner,
arrayed in pearls and pure white robes,
and at each girl's breast, fastened and fixed,
a delightful pearl took pride of place.

1093–1152. Revelation 5:6–13.
1098–1100. Revelation 14:4: "These are they who were not defiled with women: for they are virgins. These follow the Lamb whithersoever he goeth. These were purchased from among men, the firstfruits to God and to the Lamb."

93

Wyth gret delyt thay glod in fere
On golden gatez that glent as glasse;
Hundreth thowsandez I wot ther were,
& alle in sute her livrez wasse;
Tor to knaw the gladdest chere.
The Lombe byfore con proudly passe   1110
Wyth hornez seven of red golde cler;
As praysed perlez his wedez wasse.
Towarde the throne thay trone a tras.
Thagh thay wern fele, no pres in plyt,
Bot, mylde as maydenez seme at mas,
So drogh thay forth wyth gret delyt.

94

Delyt that ther hys come encroched
To much hit were of for to melle.
Thise aldermen, quen he aproched,
Grovelyng to his fete thay felle;   1120
Legyounes of aungelez togeder voched
Ther kesten ensens of swete smelle.
Then glory & gle watz newe abroched;
Al songe to love that gay Juelle;

93

They went together in sheer delight
through golden streets that gleamed like glass.
A hundred thousand I counted there,
all of them dressed in identical clothes—
it was hard to say which face was the happiest.
Proudly leading the procession was the Lamb,   1110
with seven horns of glaring gold,
His robes comprised of priceless pearls.
Those thousands traveled toward the throne,
and never once pushed, despite their numbers,
but as mild as maidens going to mass
they moved along with delightful manners.

94

The delirious delight His coming occasioned
would indeed be difficult to describe in full.
All the aldermen, upon His approach,
prostrated themselves at the Lord's feet.   1120
Legions of angels, summoned as one,
scattered their sweet-smelling incense about.
Then glory and gladness resounded again
as praises were sung to the precious Jewel

1106. Revelation 21:21: "And the twelve gates are twelve pearls, one to each: and every several gate was of one several pearl. And the street of the city was pure gold, as it were transparent glass."
1107. Revelation 5:11: "And I beheld, and I heard the voice of many angels round about the throne, and the living creatures, and the ancients; and the number of them was thousands of thousands."

The steven moght stryke thurgh the urthe to helle,
That the Vertues of heven of joye endyte.
To love the Lombe his meyny in melle
Iwysse I laght a gret delyt.

95

Delit the Lombe for to devise
Wyth much mervayle in mynde went.   1130
Best watz he, blythest, & moste to pryse,
That ever I herde of speche spent;
So worthly whyt wern wedez hys;
His lokez symple, hymself so gent.
Bot a wounde ful wyde & weete con wyse
Anende hys hert, thurgh hyde torente;
Of his quyte syde his blod outsprent.
Alas! thoght I, who did that spyt?
Ani breste for bale aght haf forbrent
Er he therto hade had delyt.   1140

96

The Lombe delyt non lyste to wene.
Thagh he were hurt & wounde hade,
In his sembelaunt watz never sene,
So wern his glentez gloryous glade.
I loked among his meyny schene,
How thay wyth lyf wern laste & lade;
Then saw I ther my lyttel quene,

by the Virtues of Heaven, whose joyful voices
might pierce the earth and penetrate hell.
Carried away by that stirring chorus
I delighted in declaring my love for the Lamb.

95

My delight in gazing at the Lamb in His glory
caused much amazement and wonder in my mind.   1130
He was perfect, unimpaired, and more worthy of praise
than any tongue could ever tell of.
The clothes He wore were wonderfully white,
His looks graceful, His demeanor gracious.
But an open wound, wide and weeping
could be seen by His heart where the skin was skewered,
and blood poured from His punctured side.
Alas, I thought; who inflicted such injury?
Any heart would sooner be scorched by sorrow
than take delight from so dark a deed.   1140

96

No one doubted the Lamb's delight;
although He was hurt by that heinous wound
He suffered in silence, displayed no pain.
In all His glances He was wonderfully glad.
And the faces of all His glorious followers
were alive with life, lit by love.
Then looking, I saw there my little queen,

That I wende had standen by me in sclade.
Lorde, much of mirthe watz that ho made,
Among her ferez that watz so quyt! 1150
That syght me gart to thenk to wade
For luf-longyng in gret delyt.

who I thought was standing on the shore of this stream.
Lord, how happy and at peace she appeared,
so pure and content among her companions. 1150
And instantly I wanted to wade that water,
longing for her, the delight of my life.

XX

97

Delyt me drof in yghe & ere;
My manez mynde to maddyng malte;
Quen I saw my frely, I wolde be there,
Beyonde the water thagh ho were walte.
I thoght that nothyng mygh me dere
To fech me bur & take me halte;
& to start in the strem schulde non me stere,
To swymme the remnaunt, thagh I ther swalte.   1160
Bot of that munt I watz bitalt;
When I schulde start in the strem astraye,
Out of that caste I watz bycalt;
Hit watz not at my Pryncez paye.

98

Hit payed hym not that I so flonc
Over mervelous merez, so mad arayde;
Of raas thagh I were rasch & ronk,
Yet rapely therinne I watz restayd.
For, ryght as I sparred unto the bonc,

XX

97

Delight deluged my eyes and ears
till my mortal mind was dizzied by madness.
Nothing mattered more than being near her.
I wanted to join her over the water
and no one would halt me, hold me back
or stop me summoning every morsel of strength
and swimming that stream. I would cross the current
or die trying and drown in its depths.   1160
But suddenly that notion was snatched away;
as the brook beckoned and I bounded forward
my bold intent was abruptly blocked:
my plan was not to the Prince's pleasing.

98

My Prince was displeased that I had approached
that teeming flood in a state of frenzy.
Rashly I had rushed toward the river
but suddenly felt a restraining force,
and just as I leapt from land to stream

That brath the out of my drem me brayde.   1170
Then wakned I in that erber wlonk,
My hede upon that hylle watz layde
Ther as my perle to grounde strayd.
I raxled & fel in gret affray,
&, sykyng, to myself I sayd,
'Now al be to that Pryncez paye.'

99

Me payed ful ille to be outfleme
So sodenly of that fayre regioun,
Fro alle tho syghtez so quyke & queme.
A longeyng hevy me strok in swone,   1180
& rewfully thenne I con to reme:
'O perle,' quod I, 'of rych renoun,
So watz hit me dere that thou con deme
In thys veray avysyoun!
If hit be veray & soth sermoun,
That thou so strykez in garlande gay,
So wel is me in thys doel-doungoun,
That thou art to that Prynsez paye.'

100

To that Pryncez paye hade I ay bente,
& yerned no more then watz me geven,   1190
& halden me ther in truwe entent,
As the perle me prayed that watz so thryven,
As helder drawen to Goddez present,

my stunt startled me out of my dream.   1170
I woke in the same green garden again
with my head laid on the little hill
where my priceless pearl had disappeared.
Roused from sleep all my sadness resumed,
and sinking in sorrow I said to myself,
'Let this be pleasing to my Prince's pleasure.'

99

It deprived me of pleasure and caused me pain
to be cast so quickly from that fair country,
exiled from all its exquisite sights.
My heart labored with a heavy longing   1180
and I cried out loud in mournful lament:
'Oh pearl,' I said, 'so high in honor.
To hear your voice in that hallowed vision
meant more to me than anything on earth.
If all that tripped from your tongue holds true
and you walk in whiteness wearing the crown
then I'll happily dwell in this dungeon, knowing
what part you play in pleasing the Prince.'

100

Had I put His pleasure before my own,
and yearned only for what was yielded,   1190
and acted only with honest intent,
and done as my perfect pearl had pleaded,
then I might have lingered longer in His presence

To mo of his mysterys I hade ben dryven.
Bot ay wolde man of happe more hente
Then moghten by ryght upon hem clyven.
Therfore my joye watz sone toriven,
& I kaste of kythez that lastez aye.
Lorde, mad hit arn that agayn the stryven,
Other proferen the oght agayn thy paye!   1200

To pay the Prince other sete hym saghte
Hit is ful ethe to the god Krystyin;
For I haf founden hym, bothe day & naghte,
A God, a Lorde, a Frende ful fyin.
Over this hyul this lote I laghte,
For pyty of my perle enclyin,
& sythen to God I hit bytaghte,
In Krystez dere blessyng & myn,
That, in the forme of bred & wyn,
The preste us schewez uch a daye.   1210
He gef us to be his homly hyne,
Ande precious perlez unto his pay. Amen. Amen.

and witnessed more of His mystery and wonder.
But a fellow will always seek further fortune;
I reached for more than was mine by right,
and that glimpse of life in the land everlasting
was shattered in a moment and the gates slammed shut.
Lord, they are mad who meddle with your laws
or propose to spoil a Prince's pleasure.   1200

101

To please the Prince and join Him in peace
is the simple choice for His faithful flock,
for day and night He has never been less
than a God, a Lord, and a loving friend.
Here on this mound this happened to me:
at first I pined for my fallen pearl,
then gave her up to go to her God,
with my blessing, and also the blessing of Christ,
who the priests prove to us time after time,
His body as bread, His blood as wine.   1210
May we live both as His lowly servants
and beautiful pearls, pleasing to Him. Amen. Amen.

Acknowledgments

I am extremely grateful to James Simpson, Donald P. and Katherine B. Loker Professor of English at Harvard University, for his encouragement and support throughout this translation, for his expert judgment and invaluable suggestions during the later drafts of the manuscript, and for kindly supplying the biblical citations that appear in this edition.

The edition of the original poem printed in parallel to this translation is that of Charles G. Osgood (1908), with spelling lightly modernized. My source texts were the edition and notes of J. J. Anderson (Everyman, revised 1996), and Malcolm Andrew and Ronald Waldron's *The Poems of the Pearl Manuscript* (Exeter Press, fourth edition, 2002), as well as *The Poems of the Pearl Manuscript in Modern English Prose Translation* (Exeter Press, 2008) by the same authors. Other works that have proved useful reference points include *A Companion to the Gawain-Poet* edited by Derek Brewer and Jonathan Gibson (D. S. Brewer, Cambridge, 1997) and editions and translations by Marie Borroff, J. R. R. Tolkien, E. V. Gordon, Jane Draycott, and William Vantuono. Thanks also to the British Library for allowing me to see the original manuscript many years ago, and to my editors at Faber & Faber in the UK and Norton in the U.S. for commissioning and overseeing this publication.